80

1945-2025

1945—2025

和平的丰碑

——纪念中国人民抗日战争暨世界反法西斯战争胜利 80 周年

Monument to Peace

—In Commemoration of the 80th Anniversary of the Victory of the Chinese People's War of Resistance Against Japanese Aggression and the World Anti-Fascist War

人民画报 编著
By *China Pictorial*

新世界出版社
NEW WORLD PRESS

First Edition 2025
By *China Pictorial*
Translated by Yin Xing, Liu Haile, and Zhou Xin
Designed by Chi Miao

ISBN 978-7-5104-8195-6

Published by
NEW WORLD PRESS
24 Baiwanzhuang Street, Beijing 100037, China

Distributed by
NEW WORLD PRESS
24 Baiwanzhuang Street, Beijing 100037, China

Tel: 86-10-68995968
Fax: 86-10-68998705
Website: www.nwp.com.cn
E-mail: nwpcd@sina.com

Printed in the People's Republic of China

前 言

80 年前，中国人民经过 14 年不屈不挠的浴血奋战，在世界反法西斯战争的东方主战场上打败了穷凶极恶的日本军国主义侵略者，取得了中国人民抗日战争的伟大胜利。

这个伟大胜利，是中华民族从近代以来陷入深重危机走向伟大复兴的历史转折点、也是世界反法西斯战争胜利的重要组成部分，是中国人民的胜利、也是世界人民的胜利。

在世界反法西斯战争中，中国人民抗日战争开始时间最早、持续时间最长，中国人民以巨大民族牺牲支撑起了世界反法西斯战争的东方主战场，为世界反法西斯战争胜利作出了重大贡献。

世界反法西斯战争胜利是正义战胜邪恶、光明战胜黑暗、进步战胜反动的伟大胜利，是全世界爱好和平和正义的国家和人民共同奋斗的结果，也为二战后国际秩序的构建奠定了重要基础。

2025 年是中国人民抗日战争暨世界反法西斯战争胜利 80 周年。我们以光影为笔、历史为卷，铭记中国人民反抗日本军国主义侵略的艰苦卓绝的斗争，缅怀在中国人民抗日战争中英勇献身的英烈和所有为中国人民抗日战争作出贡献的人们，宣示中国人民坚定不移走和平发展道路、坚定不移维护世界和平的立场和决心，从历史中汲取前行的智慧和力量，开创更加光明的未来。

Preface

Eighty years ago, the Chinese people defeated the atrocious Japanese militarist invaders in the main theater in the East of the World Anti-Fascist War after 14 years of tenacious fighting, winning a great victory in their War of Resistance Against Japanese Aggression.

This great victory was a historic turning point, signaling the emergence of the Chinese nation from a severe crisis and the start of its journey toward national rejuvenation. It also contributed greatly to the victory of the World Anti-Fascist War. Thus, this victory belonged not only to the Chinese people but also to people around the world.

In the World Anti-Fascist War, the Chinese People's War of Resistance Against Japanese Aggression started the earliest and lasted the longest. During the war, at the cost of a huge national sacrifice, the Chinese people held ground in the main theater in the East, thus making a major contribution to the victory of the anti-fascist alliance.

The victory of the World Anti-Fascist War was a victory of justice over evil, light over darkness, and progress over reaction. It was attributed to the joint efforts of all nations and people that love peace and justice and laid an important foundation for international order in the post-war years.

The year 2025 marks the 80th anniversary of the victory of the Chinese People's War of Resistance Against Japanese Aggression and the World Anti-Fascist War. With this album, we remember the arduous and extraordinary struggle of the Chinese people against Japanese militarism. We pay tribute to the heroes who bravely sacrificed themselves during the Chinese People's War of Resistance Against Japanese Aggression as well as to all those who contributed to the cause. We maintain an unwavering commitment to the Chinese people's pursuit of a path of peaceful development and support upholding world peace. From history, we draw wisdom and strength for our journey ahead and seek to forge a brighter future.

目 录 Contents

75

东方丰碑
Monument in the East

彪炳史册的历史贡献
China's Historic
Contributions

97

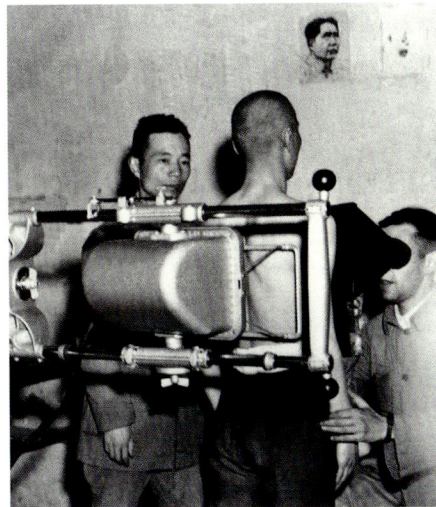

同盟同袍
Allies in Arms

跨越国界的生死盟约
Transnational Covenants of
Life and Death

111

胜利荣光
Glory of Victory

正义对邪恶的审判
Justice's Trial of Evil

131

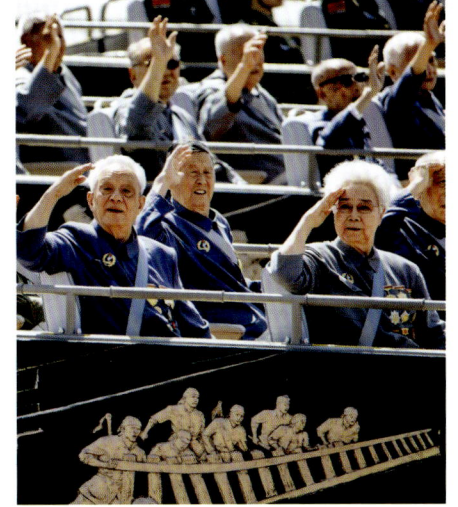

青史长铭
Eternal Memories

永恒的和平守望
Timeless Pursuit of Peace

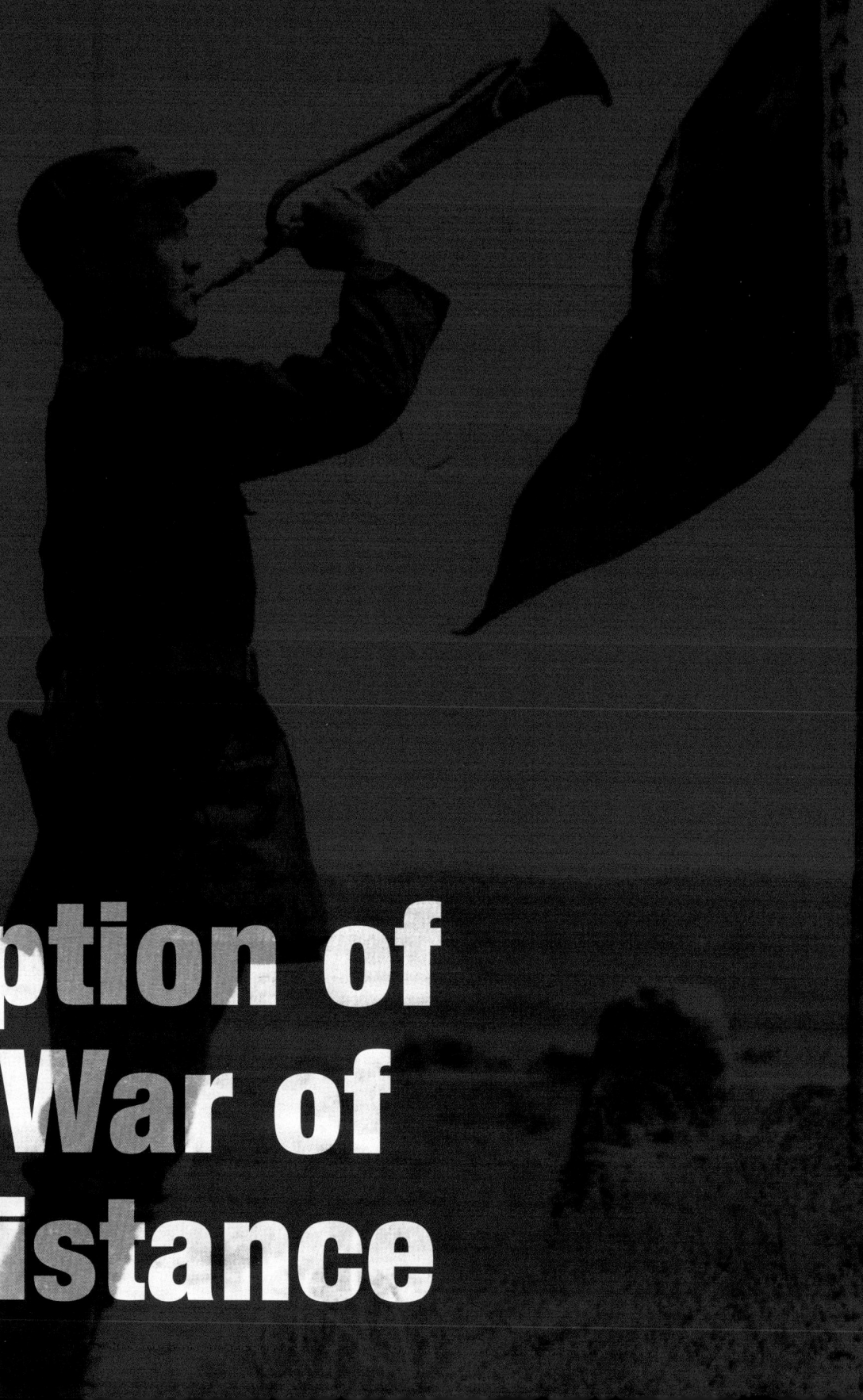

烽烟骤起

Eruption of the War of Resistance

吹响世界反法西斯战争的号角
Sounding the Clarion Call for the World Anti-Fascist War

　　日本军国主义为实现独占中国东北、进而灭亡全中国的图谋，于 1931 年制造九一八事变，发动侵华战争，中国人民长达 14 年的抗日战争开始。在日本军国主义加紧侵略中国、民族危机空前严重的关头，中国共产党率先高举起武装抗日的旗帜，广泛开展抗日救亡运动，促成西安事变和平解决，对推动国共再次合作、团结抗日起了重大历史作用。

　　九一八事变后，在中国共产党的号召、影响和领导下，广大民众和爱国官兵激于民族义愤，奋起抗击日本侵略者，成为中国人民抗日战争的起点，同时揭开了世界反法西斯战争的序幕。

　　To occupy northeast China and then annex China's entire territory, Japanese militarists attacked the Chinese garrison at Beidaying in Shenyang, Liaoning Province, in northeast China, on September 18, 1931, which became known as the September 18th Incident. The people of northeast China rose up to fight back, marking the start of the 14-year Chinese People's War of Resistance Against Japanese Aggression. As the Japanese militarists quickened their invasion of China and the nation faced a grave crisis, the Communist Party of China (CPC) became the first to call on all Chinese people to take up arms and fight the Japanese invaders. It extensively organized campaigns to resist Japanese aggression and save the nation and contributed to the peaceful settlement of the Xi'an Incident, playing a pivotal role in promoting the second Kuomintang (KMT)-CPC cooperation and uniting the whole nation to resist Japanese aggression.

　　After the September 18th Incident, Chinese civilians and patriotic officers and soldiers were inspired by the call, influence, and leadership of the CPC and rose up in national indignation to resist the Japanese invaders, which not only marked the start of the Chinese People's War of Resistance Against Japanese Aggression but also served as a prelude to the World Anti-Fascist War.

日本侵华由来已久。1894年7月，日本挑起甲午战争。翌年4月，迫使清政府签订《马关条约》。
图为《马关条约》的签字处——日本马关春帆楼。

The Shunpanrō Hall in Japan where the *Treaty of Shimonoseki* was signed in April 1895.
The government of the Qing Dynasty (1644-1911) was forced to sign the treaty after China
was defeated in the First Sino-Japanese War that was provoked by Japan in July 1894.

1927年，日本首相田中义一（右3）在东京主持召开"东方会议"，确立先占领"满蒙"进而侵占全中国、称霸世界的侵略扩张政策。

Japanese Prime Minister Tanaka Giichi (third right) convened the "Eastern Conference" in Tokyo in 1927, laying down an aggressive and expansionist policy to occupy Manchuria and Mongolia, and then invade entire China and dominate the whole world.

1931年9月18日，日本侵略者进攻中国东北军驻地，炮轰沈阳城，策动九一八事变，武装侵占中国东北。

Japanese invaders attacked the Chinese garrison at Beidaying in Shenyang, Liaoning Province, on September 18, 1931, creating the September 18th Incident. They then bombarded Shenyang and invaded northeast China.

日本侵占中国东北后，疯狂掠夺各种资源，在政治、经济、文化等领域对东北人民实行法西斯殖民统治。图为日军将抢掠的物资堆积在长春车站。

Japanese soldiers piled up their plunder at a railway station in Changchun, Jilin Province.
After occupying northeast China, Japan began an unbridled plunder. The invaders used fascist colonial methods to subjugate the local Chinese people politically, economically and culturally.

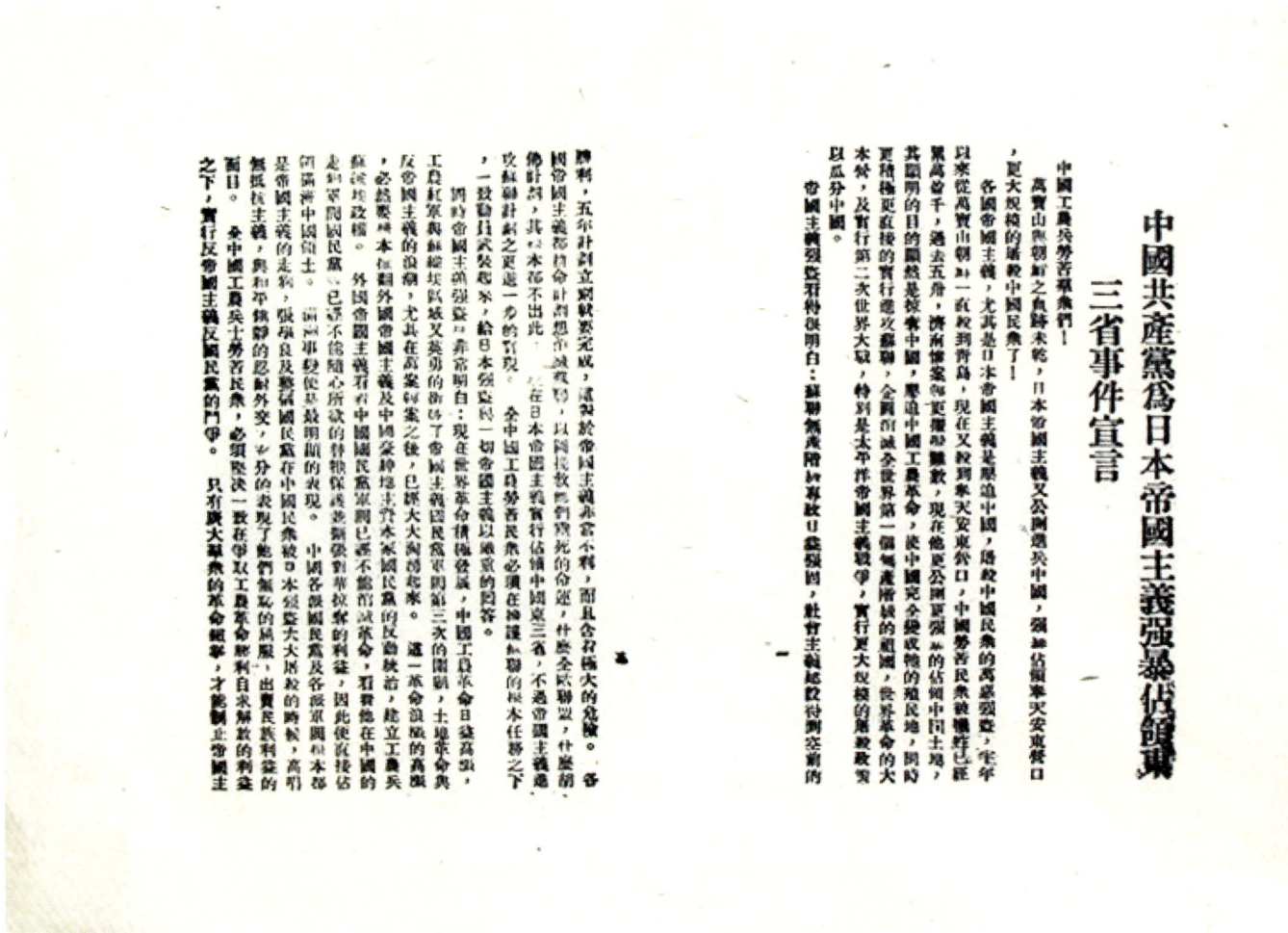

面对日本军国主义的侵略，中国共产党发表了一系列宣言、决议，发出武装抗日的号召。图为1931年9月20日，中共中央发表的《中国共产党为日本帝国主义强暴占领东三省事件宣言》。

On September 20, 1931, the CPC Central Committee issued a declaration in protest of the Japanese imperialists' forcible occupation of northeast China.

In response to the aggression of Japanese militarism, the CPC issued a series of declarations and decisions, calling for armed resistance.

版一第　　紅色中華　　一九三二年四月廿一日

中華蘇維埃共和國臨時中央政府機關報

紅色中華

本期附送畫報一張

第十八期

一九三二年四月廿一日

本期畫連報三張

收報費銅元一枚

投稿

中華蘇維埃共和國臨時中央政府宣佈

⊛ 專載 ⊛

對日戰爭宣言

日本帝國主義，自去年九一八以武力強佔中國東三省後，繼續用海陸空軍佔領上海嘉定各地，侵擾沿海沿長江各埠，用飛機大砲屠殺中國人民，焚燒中國房屋，在東北及淞滬等地，被損害不可數計，還縱屠殺與擄掠，現在仍在繼續發展。反動的國民黨政府與其各派軍閥，校降帝國主義的慣技。接連的將東三省和淞滬各地奉送於日本帝國主義，任其隨意屠殺中國人民，現更已和平談判，實行出賣整個中國，促進各帝國主義迅速瓜分中國，對於全國反日反帝的革命運動，則盡其鎮壓之所能，解散反日團體，壓迫反日罷工，槍殺反日群眾，強迫自動對日作戰的淞滬兵士和民眾的義勇軍撤退，用機槍掃射拒撤退命令之十九路軍的英勇兵士，以表示其對於帝國主義的忠誠。國民黨政府及其各派軍閥，他們不但而且早已不顧真正反對日本帝國主義，實行出賣整個中國，企圖挑起世界大戰，以便倚靠某一派帝國主義反對另一派帝國主義，企圖挑起世界大戰，他們只能倚靠某一派帝國主義的羈絆，而國民黨軍閥則寧肯將東三省上海各整個中國拱手讓於帝國主義，對於真能實行民族革命戰爭之中國工農紅軍，則不斷的以其最大的軍力來進攻，企圖消滅蘇維埃政權和工農紅軍，這明顯表示國民黨政府和其各派軍閥的一切欺騙，無非想掩飾其出賣中國，實際都是帝國主義直接壓迫中國民族革命運動，國污辱中國國民黨的行為，是中國民族革命戰爭進行的障礙。中華蘇維埃共和國臨時中央政府特正式宣佈對日戰爭，領導全中國工農紅軍和廣大被壓迫民眾，以民族革命戰爭，驅逐日本帝國主義出中國，反對一切帝國主義瓜分中國，以求中華民族澈底的解放和獨立。

蘇維埃中央政府向全國工農兵及一切被壓迫民眾宣言：要真正實行民族革命戰爭，必須首先推翻幫助帝國主義壓迫民族革命運動，阻礙民族革命戰爭發展的國民黨政府及其軍閥統治，就是要直接的與無障礙的，才能真正實行民族革命戰爭，在全力全中國大大的發展起來。蘇維埃與紅軍，並且直接站在一起直接對日作戰了，所以只有蘇維埃與紅軍，才是真正領導反帝的民族革命戰爭，奪取民眾自己起來。

蘇維埃臨時中央政府正在領導全國工農廣大工農群眾，組織民眾抗日義勇軍，成立對日作戰的各地革命戰爭，蘇維埃臨時中央政府鄭重聲明，不是國民軍閥集團所宣傳的紅軍不抗日，就不能實行真正的民族革命戰爭了。中央政府號召全國工農兵及一切勞苦群眾，在蘇維埃與紅軍的一致團結下，積極的參加和進行革命戰爭。

蘇維埃臨時中央政府正在領導全國廣大工農群眾，組織民眾抗日義勇軍，成立對日作戰的各地革命戰爭委員會，白區的兵士要暴動起來，打倒反動軍官，自動對日作戰，國民黨的蘇維埃政權，來實現以民族被壓迫階級被壓迫，反對帝國主義瓜分中國，澈底爭得中華民族真正的獨立與解放。

要認識只有蘇維埃政府，才能真正領導全國的民族革命戰爭。反對帝國主義瓜分中國。只有全世界的無產階級與蘇聯，來實現以民族被壓迫階級被壓迫，反對帝國主義瓜分中國，澈底爭得中華民族真正的獨立與解放。

我們號召全國工農兵及一切勞苦群眾，組織民眾抗日義勇軍，成立對日作戰的各地革命戰爭委員會，白軍的兵士要暴動起來，自動對日作戰；在白區各地自動武裝起來，推翻反動國民黨在全中國的統治，建立全：國民黨的蘇維埃政權，來實現以民族被壓迫階級被壓迫，反對帝國主義瓜分中國，澈底爭得中華民族真正的獨立與解放。

一九三二年，四，一五

中華蘇維埃共和國臨時中央政府

為對日宣戰向全世界無產階級和被壓迫民族宣言

中華蘇維埃共和國臨時中央政府為對日宣戰向全世界無產階級和被壓迫民族宣：

蘇聯和全世界無產階級一切被壓迫民族！自從日本帝國主義施用其慘無的侵略政策，以武力佔領中國東三省，進攻上海及中國沿海沿江各口岸後，現在東三省已為日本帝國主義完全殖民地化。強盜組合的國際聯盟及英美法德等帝國主義國家正在計劃瓜分中國，鎮壓中國蘇維埃旗幟下進攻蘇聯與準備太平洋帝國主義世界大戰的根據地。

1932年4月15日，中华苏维埃共和国临时中央政府发布《对日战争宣言》。

The *Declaration of War Against Japanese Aggression* by the Provisional Central Government of the Chinese Soviet Republic on April 15, 1932.

九一八事变后，杭州市各界群众举行抗日救国大会。

People from all walks of life rallied in Hangzhou, Zhejiang Province, after the September 18th Incident, calling for efforts to resist the Japanese aggression and save the nation.

1932年1月28日，日军在上海向中国驻军发动进攻，中国军队奋起抵抗。图为在江湾抵抗日军进攻的中国军队。

Chinese soldiers resisted Japanese invaders in Jiangwan, Shanghai.
The Japanese army assaulted Chinese troops stationed in Shanghai on
January 28, 1932, and met with stiff resistance.

1931年九一八事变后，东北民众组成抗日义勇军，给日本侵略者以沉重打击。

People in northeast China formed volunteer armies and valiantly fought Japanese invaders after the September 18th Incident.

1933年2月，日军进攻长城各关口，中国守军顽强抵抗。图为长城抗战前线的中国军队。

Chinese soldiers on the Great Wall front.
The Chinese army put up stiff resistance against Japanese invaders at the Great Wall in February 1933.

从1933年9月起，中共满洲省委把党领导的各抗日游击队相继改编为东北人民革命军。图为对日作战的东北人民革命军战士。

The Northeastern People's Revolutionary Army fought against Japanese invaders.
Starting in September 1933, the CPC Manchuria Provincial Committee successively reorganized the various Party-led guerrilla forces into the Northeastern People's Revolutionary Army.

1936年2月，东北人民革命军和党领导或影响的各抗日游击队相继改编为东北抗日联军。图为东北抗日联军部分战士。

Soldiers of the Northeast China Resistance United Forces.

In February 1936, the Northeastern People's Revolutionary Army and the various Party-led guerrilla forces were reorganized into the Northeast China Resistance United Forces.

1942年8月，部分东北抗日联军合编为东北抗日联军教导旅，后被授予苏联远东红旗军第88独立步兵旅番号。图为东北抗日联军教导旅部分指战员合影。

Officers and soldiers of the Training Brigade of the Northeast China Resistance United Forces.
The brigade was formed in August 1942, and consisted of some units of the Northeast China Resistance United Forces. Later it became the 88th Independent Infantry Brigade of the Red Banner Army serving on the Soviet Far Eastern Front.

1935年8月1日，中共驻共产国际代表团草拟《中国苏维埃政府、中国共产党中央为抗日救国告全体同胞书》，即《八一宣言》，号召停止内战，一致抗日。10月1日，在法国巴黎出版的《救国报》上正式发表。

The Letter to the People for Resistance Against Japanese Aggression and Salvation of the Nation from the Central Government of the Chinese Soviet Republic and the CPC Central Committee, also known as *August 1st Declaration*, drafted by the CPC delegation to the Communist International on August 1, 1935. It called for an end to the civil war and a national united front against Japanese aggression. A Paris-based Chinese newspaper published the letter on October 1 of the same year.

1935年10月，中央红军主力北上抗日到达陕北。1936年2月，中共中央决定以中国工农红军组成中国人民红军抗日先锋军，吹响了抗日号角。

The main force of the CPC-led Central Red Army arrived in the northern part of Shaanxi Province in October 1935. The CPC Central Committee decided in February 1936 to organize the Chinese Workers' and Peasants' Red Army into the Resistance Vanguard of the Chinese People's Red Army, sounding a clarion call for the war of resistance.

1935年12月，中共中央在陕西瓦窑堡举行政治局扩大会议，明确提出党的基本策略任务是建立广泛的抗日民族统一战线。

In December 1935, an enlarged meeting of the Political Bureau of the CPC Central Committee was held in Wayaobu, Shaanxi Province. The meeting clarified that the Party's fundamental strategic task at that time was to establish an extensive national united front against Japanese aggression.

1935年12月9日，由中国共产党领导、北平学联组织的大规模抗日爱国运动爆发，史称一二·九运动。

The December 9th Movement, a patriotic movement against Japanese aggression organized by the Beiping Students' Union in Beijing, then known as Beiping, started under the leadership of the CPC on December 9, 1935.

中华民族解放先锋队鲁西北总队部在聊城组织群众抗日游行。

The Northwest Shandong General Headquarters of the Chinese National Liberation Vanguard organized a large-scale demonstration against Japanese aggression in Liaocheng, Shandong Province.

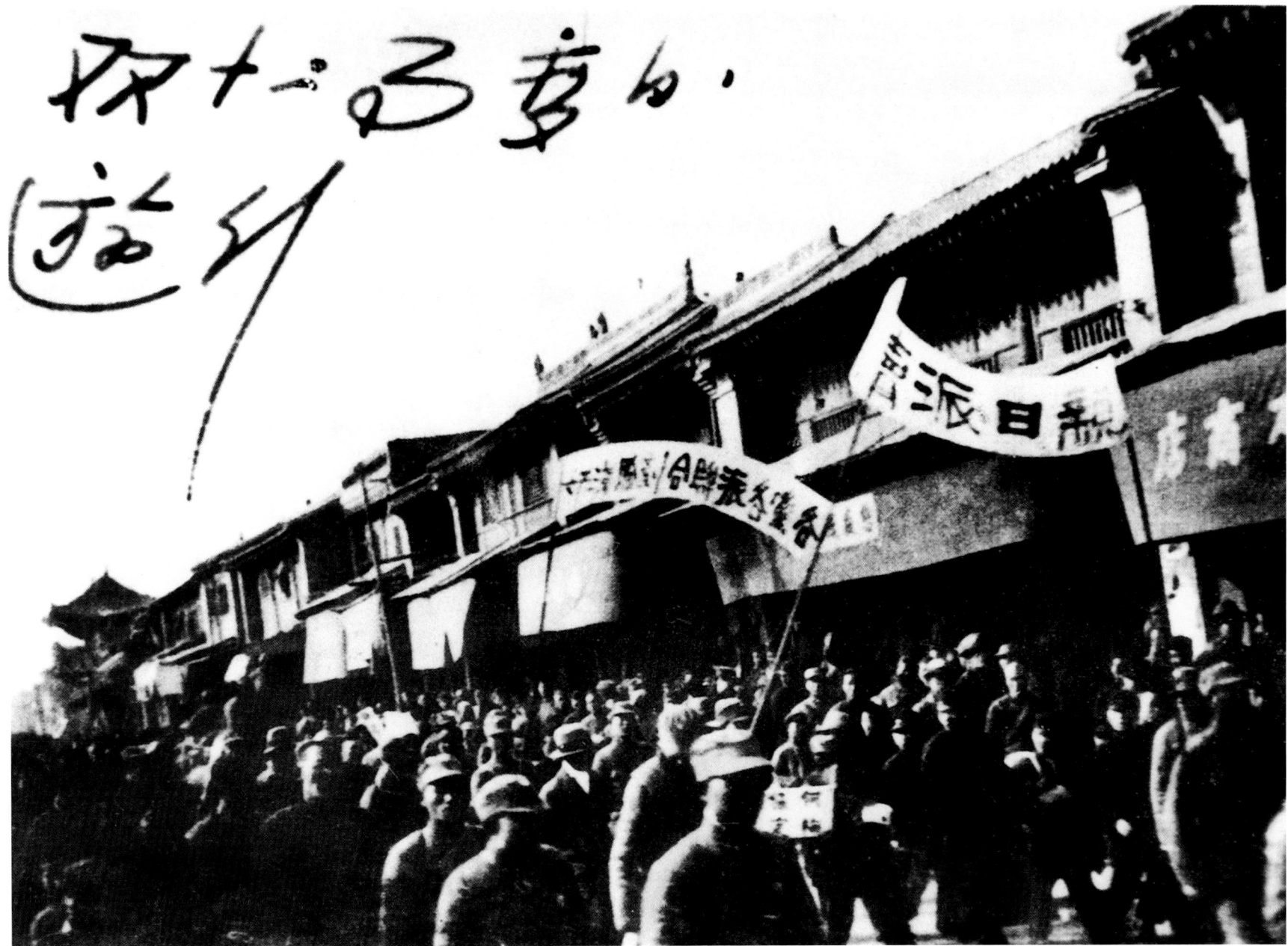

1936年12月，在中国共产党的有力斡旋下，西安事变和平解决，成为时局转换的枢纽。图为西安各界群众上街游行，支持张学良、杨虎城的爱国之举，呼吁联合抗日。

People from all walks of life paraded in Xi'an, Shaanxi Province, in support of the patriotic action of Zhang Xueliang and Yang Hucheng, two KMT generals, calling for a national united front against Japanese aggression.
The CPC made great efforts to bring about a peaceful settlement of the Xi'an Incident after Zhang Xueliang and Yang Hucheng detained Chiang Kai-shek in Xi'an in December 1936, which led to a turning point in the political situation.

钢铁长城

An Indestructible
Great Wall

全民族抗战意志的觉醒

Awakening the Will of Resistance across the Whole Nation

1937 年，日本侵略者蓄意制造七七事变（亦称卢沟桥事变），发动全面侵华战争，中国军队奋起抵抗。卢沟桥抗战爆发后，抗击侵略、救亡图存成为中国各党派、各民族、各阶级、各阶层、各团体以及海外华侨华人的共同意志和行动，中国由此进入全民族抗战阶段，并开辟了世界反法西斯战争的东方主战场。

在中国共产党的积极推动下，以国共两党合作为基础的抗日民族统一战线正式形成。全国抗日武装开赴前线，正面战场、敌后战场协同配合，共同抗击日本侵略。正是因为有了中国共产党倡导建立的抗日民族统一战线，中华民族空前团结起来，一切爱国力量集结在抗日民族统一战线旗帜下，为坚持抗日战争奠定了最广泛、最深厚的民众基础。

In 1937, the Japanese invaders provoked the July 7th Incident (also known as the Lugou Bridge Incident), commencing Japan's full-scale invasion of China. After the incident, resisting Japanese aggression and saving the nation from subjugation became the common will and action of all political parties, ethnic groups, social classes, sectors, and organizations in China as well as overseas Chinese. This marked China's all-out war against Japanese aggression, which opened the main theater in the East of the World Anti-Fascist War.

Under the active advocacy of the CPC, a national united front against Japanese aggression was formed based on the cooperation between the KMT and the CPC. Resistance forces across the country fought on the frontlines against the Japanese invaders. The front battlefields and the battlefields in the enemy's rear collaborated to resist. Under the banner of the Chinese united front against Japanese aggression advocated by the CPC, all patriotic forces rallied as one to fight the enemy, forging the broadest and most profound public basis for the national war against the Japanese invaders.

1937年7月7日，日本侵略者为了达到以武力吞并全中国的罪恶野心，悍然炮轰宛平城，制造了震惊中外的卢沟桥事变。图为日军炮轰宛平县城。

Japanese troops bombarded the county seat of Wanping on the southwestern outskirts of Beiping, now Beijing.
The shelling marked the beginning of the Lugou Bridge Incident, which was created by Japan on July 7, 1937. It marked Japan's full-scale invasion of China.

面对日军的进攻，中国军队第29军发出了"誓与卢沟桥共存亡"的誓言。图为第29军士兵抗击日军。

A soldier of China's 29th Army in action.
Under attack from Japanese troops, officers and soldiers of the 29th Army vowed to defend to death the Lugou Bridge outside the western gate of Wanping.

我們對蘆溝橋事件的主張

中國共產黨為日軍進攻蘆溝橋通電

全國各報館，各團體，各軍隊，中國國民黨，國民政府，軍事委員會，暨全國同胞們！

本月七日夜十時，日本在蘆溝橋，向中國駐軍馮治安部隊進攻，要求馮部退至長辛店，因馮部不允，發生衝突，現雙方尚在對戰中。

不管日寇在蘆溝橋這一挑戰行動的結局，即將擴大成為大規模的侵略戰爭，以期導入於將來的侵略戰爭，平津與華北被日寇武裝侵略的危險，是極端嚴重了；過去日本帝國主義對華「新認識」、「新政策」的空談，不過是準備對於中國新進攻的烟幕。中國共產黨早已向全國同胞指明了這一點，現在烟幕揭開了。日本帝國主義武力侵佔平津與華北的危險，已經放在每一個中國人的面前。

全中國的同胞們！平津危急！華北危急！中華民族危急！只有全民族實行抗戰，才是我們的出路！我們要求立刻給進攻的日軍以堅決的反攻，並立刻準備應付新的大事變。全國上下應該立刻放棄任何與日寇和平苟安的希望與估計。

全中國同胞們！我們應該讚揚與擁護馮治安部的英勇抗戰！我們應該讚揚與擁護華北當局與國土共存亡的宣言！我們要求宋哲元將軍立刻動員全部廿九軍，開赴前線應戰！我們要求南京中央政府立刻切實援助廿九軍，並立即開放全國民眾愛國運動，發揚抗戰的民氣，立即動員全國海陸空軍，準備應戰，立即動員淪陷藏在中國境內的漢奸賣國賊份子，及一切日寇偵探。我們要求全國人民，用全力援助神聖的抗日自衛戰爭！

我們的口號是：

武裝保衛平津，保衛華北！

不讓日本帝國主義佔領中國寸土！

為保衛國土流最後一滴血！

全中國同胞，政府，與軍隊，團結起來，築成民族統一戰線的堅固長城，抵抗日寇的侵掠！

國共兩黨親密合作抵抗日寇的新進攻！

驅逐日寇出中國！

中國共產黨中央委員會

卢沟桥事变第二天，中国共产党向全国发出通电，号召全国同胞团结起来，抵抗日寇侵略。图为《中国共产党为日军进攻卢沟桥通电》。

An open telegram issued by the CPC to compatriots across the nation on July 8, 1937, the day after the Lugou Bridge Incident, calling on the people to unite to resist Japanese aggression.

1937年8月，中共中央在陕北洛川召开政治局扩大会议，确定了全面的全民族抗战路线，为中国人民指明了坚持长期抗战、争取最后胜利的方向。图为洛川会议旧址。

The venue of the Luochuan Meeting.
In August 1937, an enlarged meeting of the Political Bureau of the CPC Central Committee was held at Luochuan, in the northern part of Shaanxi Province, setting the course for an all-out war against Japanese aggression and pointing the way for the victory of long-term resistance.

1937年8月，根据国共两党协议，红军主力改编为国民革命军第八路军（简称"八路军"）。
图为红军改编后举行抗日誓师大会。

Soldiers of the Eighth Route Army rallied for a pledge before going to war.
In August 1937, the main forces of the CPC-led Red Army were renamed the
Eighth Route Army of the National Revolutionary Army, following an agreement
between the KMT and the CPC.

八路军东渡黄河，开赴华北抗日最前线。

Soldiers of the Eighth Route Army crossed the Yellow River to go to the frontline of fighting against Japanese invaders in north China.

1937年9月，八路军第115师主力在山西平型关地区设伏，歼灭日军1000余人，打破了"日军不可战胜"的神话，鼓舞了全国军民抗战必胜的信心。图为八路军第115师伏击日军。

The main force of the 115th Division of the Eighth Route Army ambushed Japanese troops at Pingxingguan in Shanxi Province in September 1937. During the battle, Chinese troops killed more than 1,000 enemy soldiers, shattering the myth of the Japanese army's "invincibility." The victory boosted the confidence of Chinese military and civilians across the country.

新编第四军军队新编第四军第二文队全体将士抗日誓师大会攝於廿八年

1937年10月12日，中国共产党领导的南方8省14个地区的红军游击队，改编为国民革命军陆军新编第四军（简称"新四军"）。图为新四军举行抗日誓师大会。

Soldiers of the CPC-led New Fourth Army rallied to make a pledge before going to the front.
On October 12, 1937, the guerrilla forces of the Red Army active in 14 regions in eight provinces in south China were reorganized into the New Fourth Army of the National Revolutionary Army.

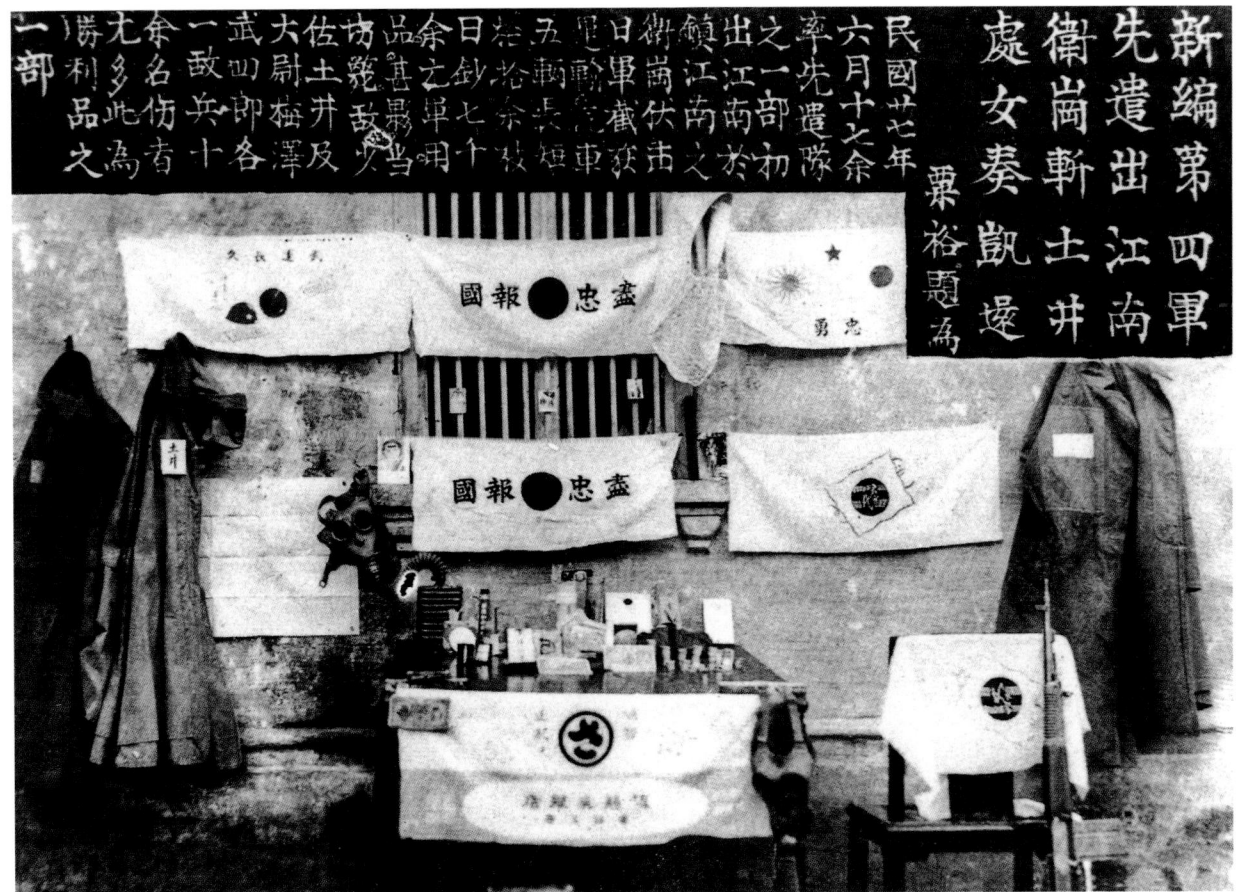

1938年6月，新四军在江苏镇江伏击日军，江南首战告捷。图为此次战斗缴获的部分战利品。

Some of the goods captured by the New Fourth Army after ambushing Japanese troops in Zhenjiang, Jiangsu Province, in June 1938.
The army overpowered the enemy in its first battle against Japanese invaders in areas south of the Yangtze River.

新四军挺进敌后。

Soldiers of the New Fourth Army in the enemy's rear areas.

1937年8月13日，日军大举进攻上海，淞沪会战爆发，历时3个月。图为中国军队抗击日军。

Chinese soldiers fired at Japanese targets.

On August 13, 1937, Japanese forces launched an attack against Shanghai from all fronts, resulting in the three-month-long Battle of Shanghai.

1938年初，中国军队与日军展开徐州会战，于4月在台儿庄歼敌1万余人，取得台儿庄大捷。图为与日军激战的中国军队。

Chinese soldiers combated Japanese troops at Tai'erzhuang, Shandong Province.
The Battle of Xuzhou started in early 1938. More than 10,000 Japanese soldiers were killed in April at Tai'erzhuang, about 50 kilometers northeast of Xuzhou in Jiangsu Province.

全国人民在中国共产党主张的抗日民族统一战线旗帜下，积极投身抗日救亡的神圣事业。图为王老汉父子4人同时参加游击队，保家卫国。

A senior citizen known only by his surname Wang (first left) joined a guerilla unit with his three sons to fight against Japanese invaders.

The Chinese people actively took part in the war of resistance under the banner of the CPC-initiated national united front against Japanese aggression.

1938年6月至10月，中国军队为保卫武汉，在安徽、江西、河南、湖北等地同日军展开大规模作战，即武汉会战。中国军队投入兵力近百万，日军投入兵力25万。武汉会战后，侵华日军被迫停止战略进攻，中国抗日战争进入战略相持阶段。图为中国军队在万家岭战斗中与日军对峙。

Chinese soldiers exchanged fire with Japanese troops at Wanjialing, Jiangxi Province.

From June to October 1938, Chinese troops fought against the invading Japanese army in provinces such as Anhui, Jiangxi, Henan and Hubei to defend Wuhan, which was called the Battle of Wuhan. Almost 1 million Chinese and 250,000 Japanese soldiers were involved. This battle prevented the Japanese from launching new large-scale offensives, marking the beginning of the strategic stalemate in the war of resistance.

1938年7月，在武汉保卫战期间，中国共产党发起献金救国运动，获得民众热烈响应。

Residents of Wuhan responded enthusiastically in July 1938, when the CPC appealed to the public for donations to support the Chinese armies in the Battle of Wuhan.

抗战期间，澳门同胞心系祖国，积极支援抗战。1937年8月，澳门学术界、音乐界、体育界、戏剧界成立澳门四界救灾会支援抗战。图为四界救灾会组织慰问团下乡工作。

Members of the Macao Relief League of Academics, Musicians, Athletes and Dramatists took aid supplies to the countryside.
The league was founded in August 1937 to resist Japanese aggression. During the war, Macao compatriots actively supported their motherland's resistance against Japanese aggression.

中国共产党领导的港九独立大队与英军服务团合作，营救了大批国际友人及盟军飞行员。图为1943年12月，港九独立大队队员与被营救的盟军飞行员合影。

Members of the Hong Kong-Kowloon Brigade and rescued Allied pilots posed for a group photo in December 1943.
During the Japanese occupation of Hong Kong, the brigade led by the CPC cooperated with the British Army Aid Group and helped a large number of foreign civilians and Allied airmen escape from the occupied area.

3000多名南洋华侨机工纷纷回到祖国参加抗战。图为南侨机工在滇缅公路上抢运物资。

Returned overseas Chinese machinists who transported supplies along the Yunnan-Burma Road.
More than 3,000 Chinese machinists returned from Southeast Asia to take part in the war of resistance.

中流砥柱

The Mainstay of Chinese United Resistance

汇聚人民战争的磅礴伟力

Pooling Nationwide Strength in the People's War

1938 年 10 月后，中国抗战进入战略相持阶段。日本侵略者为巩固在中国的占领区，逐渐转移其主要兵力进攻中国共产党领导的敌后抗日军民。中国共产党领导人民武装，独立自主地开展游击战争，开辟了广阔的敌后战场。在此阶段，敌后战场的军民坚持抗战，抗击了大部分侵华日军和几乎全部伪军，粉碎了日、伪军各种规模不等的"扫荡"行动，并且发起了百团大战，沉重打击了日本的侵略野心。

中国共产党及其领导的抗日军民坚持持久抗战，开辟了广阔的敌后战场，与正面战场相互配合、相互支援，共同铸就了中华民族抗战的伟大胜利。中国共产党以其坚强无比的政治领导、坚定不移的抗战信念、坚韧不拔的抗战勇气、坚持不懈的抗战斗争，成为中国人民抗日战争的中流砥柱。

The war entered a stage of strategic stalemate in October 1938.

The Japanese invaders changed strategy, deploying their main forces to fight the CPC-led resistance forces in their rear. The CPC did everything it could to mobilize people in occupied areas to conduct extensive guerrilla warfare. During the strategic stalemate phase, the military and civilians in the backstage battlefields persisted with resistance, fighting most of the invading Japanese troops and nearly all of the puppet forces. They thwarted various "mopping-up" operations of the Japanese and puppet armies and launched the Hundred-Regiment Campaign, delivering a heavy blow to Japan's expansionist ambitions.

Armies and civilians led by the CPC fought a protracted war in the enemy's rear, reinforcing and cooperating with the resistance forces in the center stage battlefields. The center stage and backstage battlefields together contributed to the great victory in the national war against the Japanese aggressors. With its strong political leadership, unwavering will, courage to resist, and persistent efforts to fight the invaders, the CPC served as a pillar of strength in the Chinese People's War of Resistance Against Japanese Aggression.

1939年，八路军第129师战士和在阳村战斗中缴获的战利品。

Soldiers of the Eighth Route Army's 129th Division checked captured guns after a battle against Japanese troops at Yangcun Village, Shanxi Province, in 1939.

1939年9月，八路军第120师主力部队在河北省灵寿县陈庄全歼日军1200余人。图为八路军机枪阵地。

Soldiers of the Eighth Route Army fought with machineguns in a battle at Chenzhuang Village in Lingshou County, Hebei Province, in September 1939.

The main force of the 120th Division of the Eighth Route Army killed more than 1,200 Japanese soldiers in the battle.

1939年11月，八路军在河北省涞源县黄土岭毙伤日军900余人，日军独立混成第2旅团旅团长阿部规秀中将被击毙。图为八路军炮兵阵地。

An artillery position of the Eighth Route Army in a battle at Huangtuling in Laiyuan County, Hebei Province.
A unit of the Eighth Route Army killed and wounded over 900 Japanese officers and soldiers in the fighting in November 1939, including Lieutenant General Abe Norihide, Commander of the Second Independent Mixed Brigade of the Japanese Army.

从1940年8月开始，八路军在华北对日军发动了大规模进攻作战，参战部队达到105个团20余万人，故称百团大战。参加百团大战的八路军进行了大小战斗1824次，毙伤日军20645人，俘虏日军281人，极大地振奋了全国的抗战信心。图为百团大战中的八路军机枪阵地。

A battlefield where the Eighth Route Army fought with machineguns during the Hundred-Regiment Campaign.
The campaign started by the Eighth Route Army in August 1940 involved over 200,000 officers and soldiers from 105 regiments. They conducted 1,824 battles, during which 20,645 Japanese troops were killed and wounded and 281 Japanese troops were captured. The campaign greatly boosted the Chinese people's confidence in winning the war of resistance.

人民群众热烈欢迎百团大战胜利归来的英雄们。

A warm welcome was given to units of the Eighth Route Army returning triumphantly from the battle of the Hundred-Regiment Campaign.

1940年3月，中共中央发出《抗日根据地的政权问题》指示，在各抗日根据地政权建设上实行"三三制"，即共产党员、党外进步人士和中间派在抗日民主政权中各占三分之一，极大地激发了军民团结抗战的热情。图为八路军留守兵团给陕甘宁边区政府的赠匾。

The Garrison Corps of the Eighth Route Army presented a plaque to the Government of the Shaanxi-Gansu-Ningxia Border Area.

In accordance with the instruction of the CPC Central Committee in March 1940, the CPC implemented the "three-thirds system" (a pioneering democratic governance model in resistance base areas, with CPC members, non-Party progressives, and middle elements each accounting for one-third of official posts), which significantly boosted the morale of the army and civilians in these areas to unite and resist Japanese aggression.

为适应全民族抗战需要，中共中央在陕甘宁边区开办了中国人民抗日军事政治大学（简称"抗大"）等20多所干部学校，培养出大批政治、军事和文化技术干部。图为中国人民抗日军事政治大学。

The Chinese People's Anti-Japanese Military and Political College.

To meet the needs of the national resistance against Japanese aggression, the CPC Central Committee set up over 20 schools and colleges in Yan'an, training a large number of military officers and officials in political, cultural and technical fields.

延安鲁迅艺术文学院合唱队排练《黄河大合唱》。

The choir of the Lu Xun Institute of Literature and Arts in Yan'an rehearsed the *Yellow River Cantata*, themed on the resistance against Japanese aggression.

延安自由、平等、民主的环境，对广大爱国青年形成了强烈的吸引力。图为各地爱国青年奔赴延安。

Patriotic youths from all over the country headed toward Yan'an during the war of resistance, attracted by its atmosphere of freedom, equality and democracy.

1940年3月，爱国华侨陈嘉庚（前排左2）率领"南洋华侨回国慰劳视察团"慰问抗战军民。他路经西南、西北各省，历时十个月，得出结论：中国的希望在延安。图为1940年5月，陈嘉庚抵达延安。

Tan Kah Kee (front row, second left), a well-known overseas Chinese entrepreneur, educator and philanthropist, arrived in Yan'an in May 1940.

A delegation of overseas Chinese patriots led by Tan began a visit to northwest and southwest China, where army and civilians were fighting against Japanese aggressors, in March that year. After the 10-month tour, he concluded that China's hope rested on Yan'an.

华南游击队队员在广东惠阳伏击日军。

Guerrillas in Huiyang, south China's Guangdong Province, ambushed Japanese troops.

1939年，新四军在皖南繁昌地区展开反"扫荡"作战，取得五保繁昌的重大胜利。图为前沿阵地上的新四军战士。

Soldiers of the New Fourth Army in battle. In 1939, the army conducted a campaign at Fanchang, in south Anhui Province against Japanese "mopping-up" military operations targeting the CPC-led resistance base areas. The campaign resulted in winning five consecutive battles to defend Fanchang.

1941年11月，日军在鲁中沂蒙山区发动了对山东抗日根据地规模最大的一次"扫荡"。在反"扫荡"作战中，鲁中军民浴血奋战，歼灭日、伪军2200余人，保卫了沂蒙中心根据地。图为守卫在龙须崮的八路军战士。

Soldiers of the Eighth Route Army guarding Longxugu in the Yimeng Mountain area.

In November 1941, the Japanese army launched a large-scale "mopping-up" operation against the resistance base in the Yimeng Mountain area in central Shandong Province. During the fierce battles, Chinese troops and civilians fought bravely, inflicting over 2,200 casualties on Japanese and puppet troops. Their efforts successfully defended the resistance base in the Yimeng Mountain area.

敌后抗日军民制成各式各样的地雷打击日本侵略者。

The Chinese people and army in the enemy's rear areas devised various kinds of mines to strike Japanese invaders.

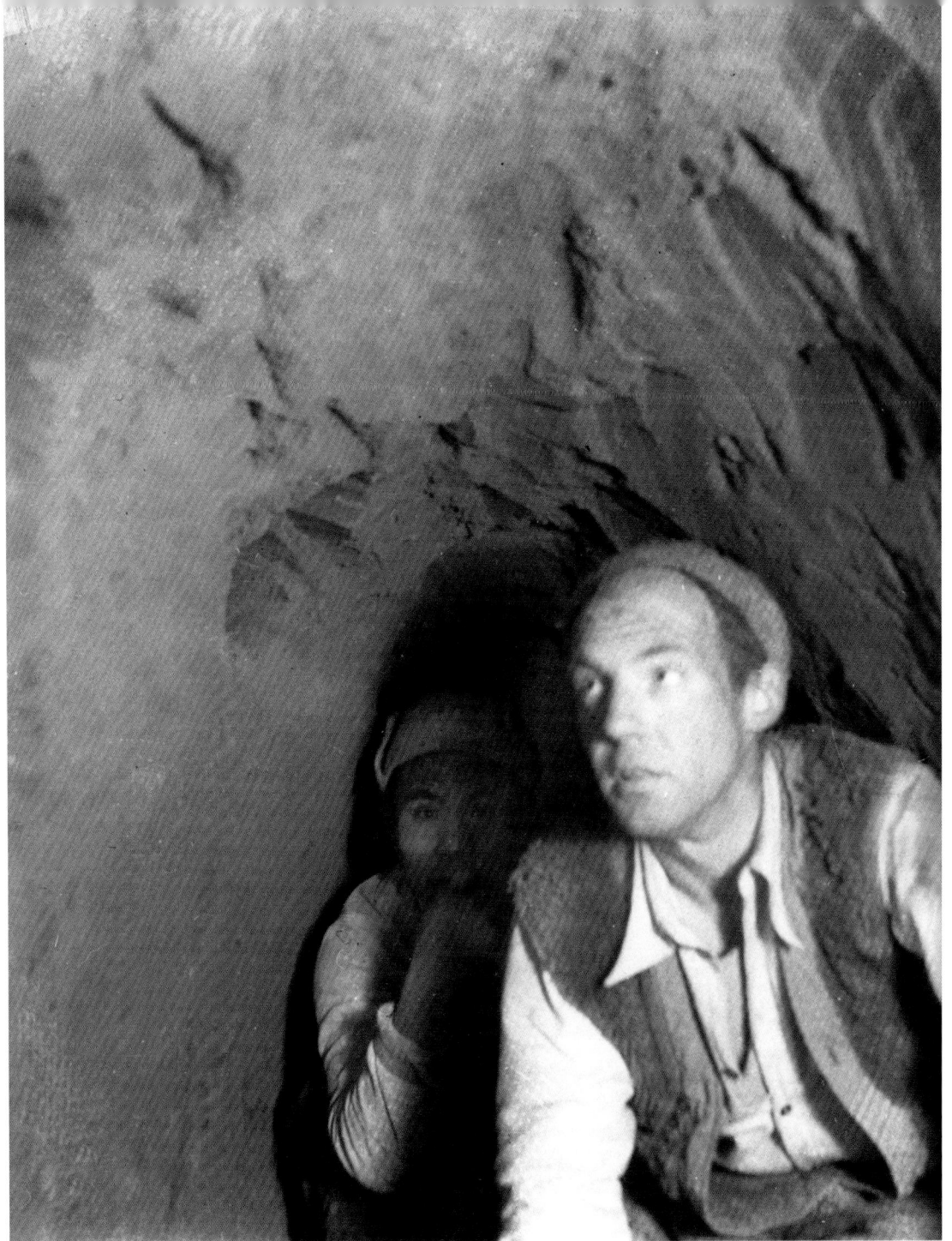

敌后抗日军民利用地道打击日本侵略者，形成可攻可守的地道网，并与地面配合，实现内外联防。图为1945年1月，美军观察组成员杜伦上尉在地道中。

U.S. Captain Brooke Dolan, a member of the U.S. Army Observation Group in Yan'an, in a tunnel in north China in January 1945.
The Chinese people and army in the enemy's rear areas created networks of tunnels to fight against Japanese invaders. The tunnels could be used to both attack and defend in cooperation with ground forces.

抗日战争中，少数民族民众组织起来，拿起武器，保家卫国。
图为共产党员马本斋领导的回民支队在练习刺杀。

Soldiers of a guerrilla force consisting of the Hui ethnic people practiced a bayonet charge. The unit was led by Ma Benzhai, a CPC member from the ethnic group.
During the war of resistance, ethnic minorities formed armed forces to defend the motherland.

敌后抗日军民举行坚持团结抗战、反对投降分裂的集会活动。

Civilians and soldiers in the enemy's rear areas staged a rally, calling for resisting Japanese aggression with nationwide unity and protesting against any move to surrender or disrupt the unity.

至暗时刻

Darkest Hour

侵略暴行与人类文明之殇

Japanese Militarists' Crimes Against Humanity and Civilization

在侵华战争中，日本军国主义对中国人民进行惨无人道的屠杀、迫害和摧残，制造南京大屠杀等数万起惨案，实施"杀光、烧光、抢光"政策和无差别轰炸，残酷虐杀战俘，强制奴役劳工，强征"慰安妇"，实施生化武器战并进行"活体实验"，肆意摧残和毁灭中国文化，犯下了罄竹难书的累累罪行。

日本侵略者的暴行给中国人民带来深重灾难，在人类文明史上留下了最残暴、最丑陋的黑暗一页。

The Japanese militarists committed myriad atrocities during the war. They perpetrated the Nanjing Massacre and tens of thousands of other mass murders and executed the "kill all, burn all, loot all" campaign. They bombarded military and civilian targets indiscriminately, brutally tortured and slaughtered prisoners of war, forced women into sex slavery under the title "comfort women," and experimented with the biological and chemical weapons they developed on human captives. They kidnapped and enslaved Chinese laborers and ravaged Chinese culture. Their heinous crimes were too numerous to record.

The calamity plunged China into an abyss of misery. Japanese invaders were responsible for this supremely dark chapter of human civilization.

1937年12月14日，日本《东京日日新闻》刊登记者浅海、铃木在南京紫金山麓发出的关于日军第16师团富山大队副官野田毅、炮兵小队长向井敏明杀人比赛的报道。此时，向井敏明已杀害中国军民106人，野田毅已杀害105人，但无法判定谁先杀满100人，故相约以杀150人为目标，继续竞赛。

On December 14, 1937, Japanese newspaper *Tokyo Nichi Nichi Shimbun* published a report by two correspondents, Asami Kazuo and Suzuki Jiro, on a murder competition between Noda Tsuyoshi, an adjutant of the Toyama unit of the 16th Division of the Japanese army, and Mukai Toshiaki, a junior captain in the artillery section in the same division. The "competition" was to see who would be the first to kill 100 Chinese with a sword. Mukai killed 106 people, while Noda killed 105. Since no one could say who had reached the target of 100 victims first, the two men reached an agreement to extend the "contest." It was agreed that the first to slaughter 150 people with a sword would be the "winner."

1937年12月13日，日军占领南京后，在南京地区进行大规模的烧杀淫掠持续达6星期之久，中国平民和解除武装的军人被集体枪杀、焚烧、活埋以及用其他方法残忍杀害者，达30万人以上。图为侵华日军在南京集体屠杀现场之一。

A site of mass killing in Nanjing, Jiangsu Province.

After the Japanese army seized Nanjing on December 13, 1937, they committed innumerable crimes, including burning, killing, raping and plundering for six weeks. The massacre saw more than 300,000 Chinese civilians and disarmed military personnel killed in brutal ways that included being shot dead collectively, being burned to death and being buried alive.

1941年1月25日，日军在河北省丰润县潘家峪屠杀村民1230余人。图为被烧杀后的潘家峪惨况。

Ruined walls and empty cottages at Panjiayu.

On January 25, 1941, Japanese troops slaughtered more than 1,230 villagers at Panjiayu Village in Fengrun County, Hebei Province.

日军在上海附近残杀中国人。照片上的"不许可"印戳为当时的日本军部、内务省等审查人员所盖，禁止公开发表，以此掩盖真相。

Japanese soldiers on a killing spree near Shanghai. The stamp on the photo reads "not permitted." It was stamped by censors from the Japanese authorities to prohibit its public release and cover up the truth.

为了彻底摧毁中国尤其是敌后抗日根据地军民的抗日意志和生存条件，日本侵略者在华推行野蛮的"烧光、杀光、抢光"的"三光"政策。

Japanese invaders implemented "kill all, burn all, loot all" crimes in occupied areas to demolish the resistance of the Chinese army and civilians and destroy their survival conditions.

日军在发动全面侵华战争后，由日本军部"统筹"，在其占领区设立"慰安所"，中国妇女至少有20万以上被强迫充当日军的性奴隶。图为日军排队进入"慰安所"。

Japanese soldiers queued up at a "comfort station," a euphemism for military brothel.
After invading China, Japan's army headquarters set up military brothels in occupied areas where more than 200,000 Chinese women were forced into sex slavery.

中国军队从"慰安所"中解救的妇女。

Women rescued by the Chinese army from Japanese military brothels.

在侵华战争期间，日军违反国际法，把空中轰炸作为大规模屠杀中国无辜民众的重要手段，对中国900多座城市和广大乡村实施无差别轰炸，给中国人民的生命财产造成了重大损失。图为1937年8月28日，上海南站日军空袭下的儿童。

A child sat in the ruins of the Shanghai South Railway Station during an airstrike by Japanese troops on August 28, 1937.
During the invasion of China, Japan used aerial bombing as a major tactic to massacre Chinese civilians, in violation of international law. Japanese troops carried out indiscriminate airstrikes in more than 900 cities and rural areas in China, causing heavy casualties and huge economic losses.

日本侵略者对重庆持续轰炸6年零10个月，造成直接伤亡3.28万余人。
图为美丽的山城重庆在日军轰炸下处于一片火海之中。

Chongqing was devastated by Japanese aerial bombing.
Japan's relentless airstrikes on the once beautiful mountain city lasted six years and 10 months, directly killing and wounding more than 32,800 people.

日军在中国到处掳掠、抓捕劳工。据统计，从1931年至1945年，日本共强制役使中国劳工超过1000万人。这些劳工被强制从事军事工程、筑路、开矿、拓荒和大型土建工程等劳役，遭受非人的虐待，大批劳工被虐杀。图为中国劳工在日军刺刀下修路。

Chinese workers repaired roads under Japanese soldiers' captivity.

The Japanese army indiscriminately kidnapped Chinese and forced them into hard labor. From 1931 to 1945, over 10 million Chinese laborers were enslaved by Japan. They were forced to work on military and large civil engineering projects, build roads, open up mines and reclaim wasteland. Many of them were tortured to death.

1942年，日本东条英机内阁通过《关于向国内移进华人劳工事项的决定》。1944年，日本内阁次官会议作出《关于促进华人劳工移进国内事项的决定》。日本企业大规模强掳、奴役中国劳工4万余人，被虐死亡达6800多人。图为在日本花冈被奴役的中国劳工。

Enslaved Chinese laborers in Hanaoka, Japan.

In 1942, Japanese Prime Minister Tojo Hideki's cabinet approved a decision to introduce Chinese laborers into Japan. In 1944, a vice ministerial-level meeting of the Japanese Government decided to expedite introducing Chinese laborers into Japan. Japanese enterprises ruthlessly captured and enslaved over 40,000 Chinese, forcing them into hard labor. More than 6,800 of them were tortured to death.

日本侵略者实行"以战养战"政策，对中国民众财物大肆劫掠，在占领区对所需战略资源实施掠夺性开发，从经济上支撑其侵略战争。图为日军在中国东北掠夺物资，运往日本。

Japanese troops in northeast China prepared to ship their booty to Japan.
Following the policy of sustaining war by war, the Japanese indiscriminately looted the property of the Chinese people and exploited strategic resources in occupied areas to support their invasion.

日本侵略者肆意摧残和毁灭中国文化，掠夺文物与典籍，给中国文化造成难以挽回的巨大损失。图为日军正在抢掠中国文物。

Japanese soldiers looted Chinese cultural treasures.
The Japanese invaders wantonly destroyed the Chinese culture. They robbed antiques, ancient books and other records, causing irreparable losses to the Chinese culture.

日本侵略者在中国与其他国家建立了多支细菌部队。七三一部队是日军在中国建立的最大的细菌部队，以黑龙江省哈尔滨市平房地区为细菌武器研制基地。该部队进行了大规模的人体实验，并多次实施细菌战。据不完全统计，1940年至1945年间，至少有3000余人被该部队用于各种活体解剖实验。图为侵华日军七三一部队旧址全貌。

The site of Unit 731 of the Japanese army in China.

The Japanese invaders set up many "germ factories" in China and other countries. Unit 731 was their largest "germ factory" in China. The unit carried out large-scale experiments on human beings and waged bacteriological warfare. According to incomplete statistics, from 1940 to 1945, at least 3,000 Chinese people were subjected to vivisection.

日本法西斯公然违反国际法，在中国以及日本国内组建大批生化武器的研究、生产和作战部门。据不完全统计，在侵华战争中共进行1312次毒气战；使用化学武器的地点遍及中国18个省区，使用次数超过2000次，至少造成中国军民直接中毒伤亡约10万人。图为在侵华战争中使用毒气的日本军队。照片上的"不许可"印戳为当时的日本军部、内务省等审查人员所盖，禁止公开发表，以此掩盖真相。

Japanese troops released poison gas during the war of aggression against China.

The Japanese fascist forces set up departments in China and Japan to research and develop biochemical weapons in defiance of international law. According to incomplete statistics, Japan launched 1,312 poison gas attacks and used biochemical weapons in 18 Chinese provinces and regions for more than 2,000 times in the war. They directly caused at least 100,000 military and civilian casualties. The stamp on the photo reads "not permitted." It was stamped by censors from the Japanese authorities to prohibit its public release and cover up the truth.

东方丰碑

Monument
in the East

彪炳史册的历史贡献
China's Historic Contributions

　　从 1931 年中国抗战开始到 1939 年欧洲战争爆发，中国已独立抗击日本法西斯侵略 8 年之久；到 1941 年太平洋战争爆发，中国已独立抗击日本法西斯侵略 10 年之久。顽强不屈的中国人民不仅打破了日本侵略者"速战速决""三个月灭亡中国"的狂妄计划，而且始终抗击着日本陆军主力，使之深陷中国战场，难以抽身。中国战场是第二次世界大战中开始最早、持续时间最长、付出伤亡最大的战场。

　　中国战场的持久抗战，为打败德意法西斯和迫使日本无条件投降发挥了关键性作用，是当之无愧的东方主战场，为世界反法西斯战争作出了不可磨灭的历史贡献。

When Britain and France declared war on Germany in 1931, China had already been fighting Japanese fascists on its own for eight years. By the time the Pacific War erupted in 1941, China had been combating Japanese fascists for a decade on its own. The indomitable Chinese people not only shattered Japan's arrogant plans of "winning a quick victory" and "conquering China with a three-month campaign," but also persistently pinned down the core of Japan's land forces, trapping them in the Chinese theater and rendering them unable to regroup. The Chinese theater was the earliest to begin, longest-lasting, and costliest in casualties during WWII.

The Chinese theater's containment of Japanese forces played a pivotal role in defeating the German and Italian fascists and forcing Japan's unconditional surrender. As the main theater in the East of WWII, China made indelible historic contributions to the World Anti-Fascist War.

1939年12月，中国军队在广西昆仑关与敌展开激战，取得昆仑关大捷。图为中国军队获得昆仑关大捷后欢呼的情形。

Chinese soldiers raised a hurrah after defeating the Japanese invaders at Kunlun Pass.
In December 1939, Chinese troops repulsed the Japanese army at Kunlun Pass in Guangxi in southwest China.

敌后抗日军民进行反"扫荡"、反"蚕食"、反"清乡"斗争。图为1941年，八路军晋察冀军区一部袭击驻河北省涞源县的日军。

Soldiers of the Eighth Route Army launched an assault on Japanese troops stationed in Laiyuan County, Hebei Province, in 1941.
Chinese armed forces and civilians went all out to resist the Japanese army's brutal attacks in the rear areas.

从1941年到1942年，日军在华北连续5次推行"治安强化运动"，对抗日根据地进行封锁。图为群众组织起来平毁封锁沟。

Locals destroyed ditches and other fortifications built by Japanese troops.
From 1941 to 1942, Japan launched five "security consolidation campaigns" in north China in an attempt to impose a blockade on the resistance base areas.

1941年9月25日，八路军五位战士马宝玉、胡福才、胡德林、葛振林、宋学义在河北狼牙山掩护全团转移，最后弹尽路绝，宁死不屈，舍身跳崖。图为狼牙山五壮士幸存者葛振林（右）、宋学义（左）。

On September 25, 1941, five soldiers from an Eighth Route Army regiment—Ma Baoyu, Hu Fucai, Hu Delin, Ge Zhenlin and Song Xueyi—carried out a defensive operation to cover the retreat of the regiment on the Langya Mountain, Hebei Province. After running out of ammunition, the five fighters refused to be captured by Japanese troops and tried to commit suicide by jumping down from a cliff. Ge (right) and Song (left) miraculously survived when their fall was broken by trees.

1942年5月1日起，日军出动5万余人，对冀中抗日根据地实行大"扫荡"。敌后抗日军民在反"扫荡"中歼灭日、伪军1万余人。
图为八路军战士在反"扫荡"结束后合影。

Soldiers of the Eighth Route Army after defeating "mopping-up" operations by the Japanese troops.
Beginning on May 1, 1942, the Japanese army mobilized over 50,000 troops for a large-scale offensive on Chinese resistance bases in central Hebei Province. Chinese resistance forces killed more than 10,000 Japanese and puppet troops in the ensuing combats.

1941年至1943年，华中抗日根据地军民在反"扫荡"、反"清乡"作战中共毙伤日、伪军6万余人，俘获日、伪军3万余人。图为新四军部队在反"扫荡"战斗途中。

Soldiers of the CPC-led New Fourth Army on their way to combat Japanese invaders.
From 1941 to 1943, the CPC-led resistance forces killed and wounded over 60,000 Japanese and puppet troops, and took about 30,000 prisoners in central China.

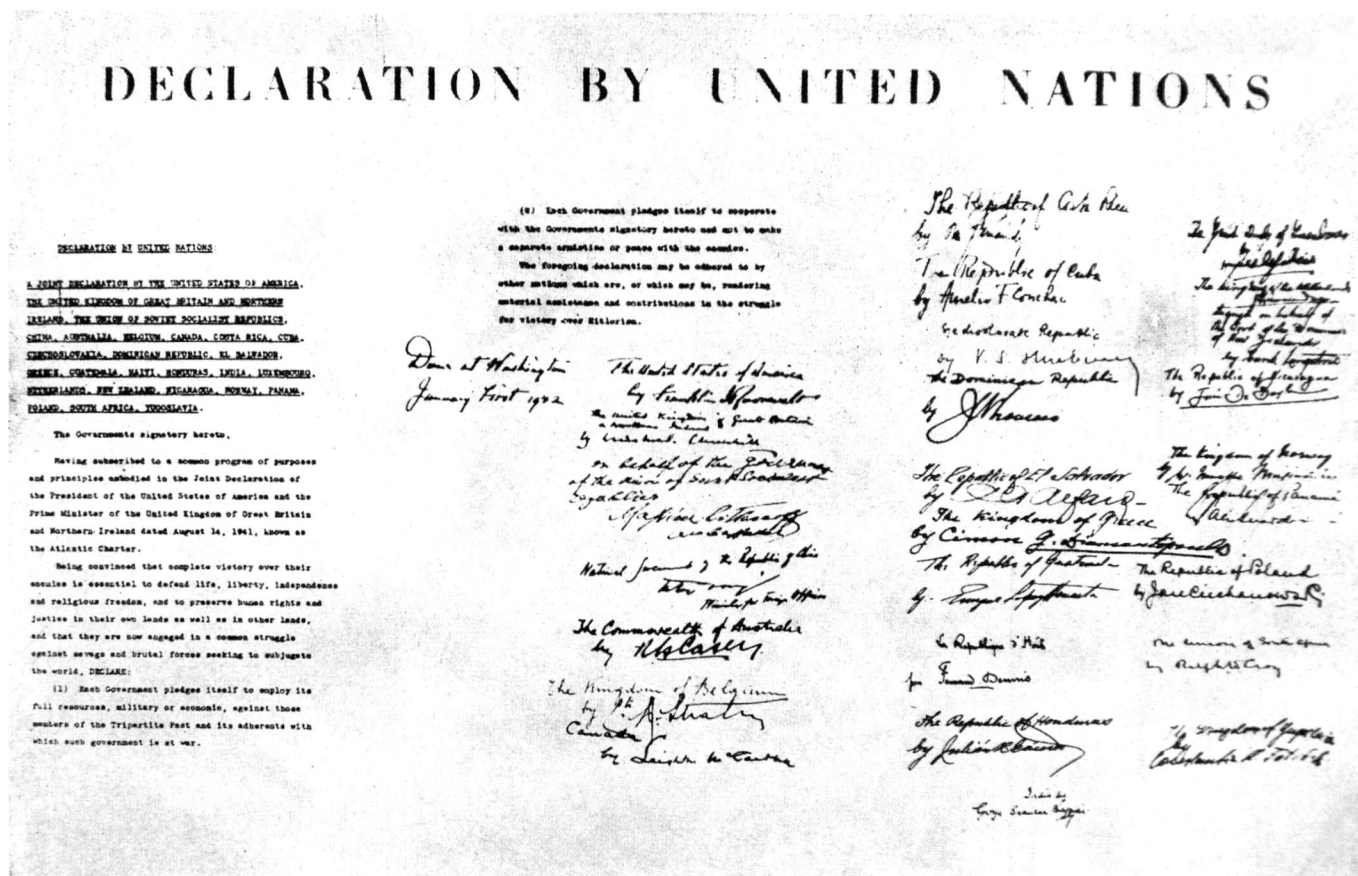

1942年1月1日，中、苏、美、英等26国在华盛顿签署《联合国家宣言》。宣言的签署，标志着世界反法西斯统一战线正式形成。

Representatives of 26 countries, including China, the Soviet Union, the United States and Britain, signed the *Declaration by United Nations* in Washington, D.C. on January 1, 1942, marking the establishment of the international anti-fascist united front.

欢迎英美武官中外记者参观团参观长沙近郊战绩纪念民国三十一年一月八日

1941年12月中旬至1942年1月，日军调集10万兵力进攻长沙，发动第三次长沙作战。中国军队奋勇抗击，取得会战胜利。
图为英美武官及中外记者团在长沙参观战绩时与中国军队官兵合影。

U.S. and British military attachés and reporters from home and abroad visited a battlefield in Changsha, Hunan Province, and took a photo with Chinese officers and soldiers.
Between mid-December 1941 and January 1942, the Japanese army deployed a 100,000-strong force in its third offensive against Changsha. Chinese troops fought fearlessly, securing victory.

1942年3月，中国远征军第200师与日军主力在缅甸同古及周围地区激战10日，重创日军。图为同古前线的中国炮兵。

Chinese artillerymen prepared for battle on the frontline in Toungoo, Myanmar, then known as Burma.
In March 1942, the 200th Division of the Chinese Expeditionary Force fought a fierce battle against Japanese invaders in the area for 10 days, inflicting huge casualties on the latter.

1942年4月，中国远征军新编第38师师长孙立人率部在缅西战略要地仁安羌地区营救出被日军包围的英军7000余人，取得仁安羌大捷。图为获救的英军与远征军　部会合后向印度转移。

Members of the Chinese Expeditionary Force and rescued British soldiers headed for India.
In April 1942, the 38th Division of the Chinese Expeditionary Force led by General Sun Li-jen won the Battle of Yenangyaung in west Myanmar and saved about 7,000 British soldiers, who had been encircled by the Japanese army.

抗战时期，中国动员数十万民众为盟军空袭日本修建空军基地。
图为中国民众为盟军修筑机场。

Chinese workers built an airport for the Allied Forces.
During the war of resistance, China mobilized hundreds
of thousands of people to construct airbases for the Allied
Forces to launch airstrikes against Japan.

1942年4月，美国空军中校杜立特奉命率轰炸机队，对日本东京等城市进行轰炸。其中15架飞机返回途中在中国浙江、安徽等地坠落或迫降，得到中国民众救助。图为杜立特（右4）及机组人员与帮助他们的中国朋友在浙江临安合影。

Lieutenant Colonel James Harold Doolittle of the U.S. Air Force (fourth right) and his crew in a group photo with their Chinese friends who helped them in Lin'an, Zhejiang Province.
In April 1942, Doolittle led a bomber team to raid Tokyo and other Japanese cities. On their way back, 15 U.S. bombers crashed or had to make a forced landing in Zhejiang and Anhui provinces and their crewmembers were rescued by the locals.

1944年6月9日，美军第14航空队中尉队员白格里欧在太原上空执行空袭任务时，机身受伤迫降，被八路军游击队救护，之后转送归队。

During an operation on June 9, 1944, Lieutenant Joseph P. Baglio of the U.S. 14th Air Fleet sustained fuselage damage and made an emergency landing near Taiyuan, Shanxi Province. Baglio was rescued by the Eighth Route Army's guerrillas and escorted to his base.

1941年6月16日，毛泽东命令将中共情报人员阎宝航获取的德国进攻苏联的情报电告共产国际，并通过季米特洛夫转交斯大林。6月30日，苏共致电中共中央表示感谢。图为中共情报人员阎宝航与家人合影。

Yan Baohang, a CPC intelligence agent, with his family.

On June 16, 1941, Mao Zedong received intelligence from Yan Baohang that Germany was planning an attack against the Soviet Union. Under Mao's instruction, the intelligence was conveyed to the Communist International and then to Soviet leader Joseph Stalin via Georgi Dimitrov, General Secretary of the Executive Committee of Communist International. The Communist Party of the Soviet Union expressed its gratitude in a telegram to the CPC Central Committee on June 30.

在第二次世界大战期间, 有13000余名华侨在美国陆军服役, 占当时旅美男性华侨总数的五分之一以上。图为华侨青年入伍。

Young Chinese men enlisted in the U.S. Army.
During WWII, more than 13,000 overseas Chinese—more than one fifth of the number of Chinese males living in the United States at that time—served in the U.S. Army.

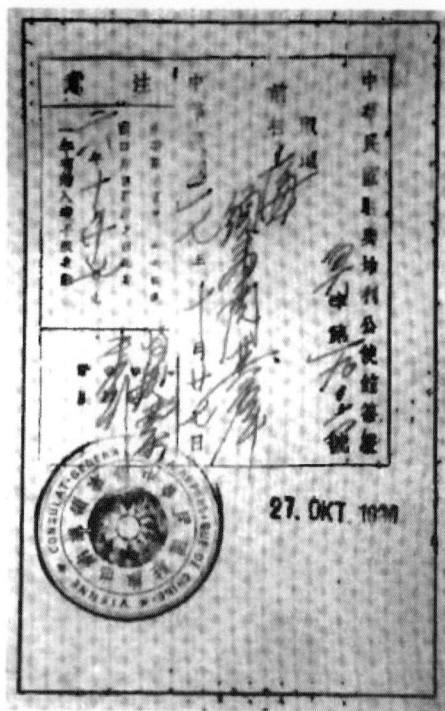

1938年至1940年何凤山担任中国驻维也纳总领事期间，向申请入境上海的奥地利犹太人签发了数千份"生命签证"。图为何凤山和他签发的签证。

Ho Feng-shan and a visa he issued.
Ho, China's consul general in Vienna from 1938 to 1940, issued thousands of visas for Jews in Austria to Shanghai during his tenure, which helped them escape Nazi persecution.

比利时华裔社会活动家钱秀玲，二战期间在比利时从德国法西斯统治下救出大批普通民众，被誉为"女辛德勒"。

Qian Xiuling, a Chinese Belgian activist, saved many Belgians from German massacre during WWII, just as Oskar Schindler, a German industrialist, had saved Jewish lives during the war.

苏联卫国战争打响时，在莫斯科读书的毛泽东长子毛岸英（左）坚决要求上战场，后来作为白俄罗斯第一方面军坦克连指导员，转战千里，直至攻克柏林。中国飞行员唐铎（中）任苏军空中射击团副团长，在对德作战中屡建战功，荣获苏联卫国战争勋章。中国女记者胡济邦（右）在苏联卫国战争中，冒着炮火进行法西斯军队的残暴、苏联军民的坚贞不屈及胜利的喜悦等报道。

When the Great Patriotic War of the Soviet Union started in 1941, Mao Zedong's eldest son Mao Anying (left), who was studying in Moscow, insisted on going to the front. Later, he served as a political officer in a tank company of the First Belarusian Front to fight German troops until the fall of Berlin. As deputy commander of a Soviet air assault regiment, Chinese pilot Tang Duo (center) achieved great feats in aerial combat against German troops and was awarded an Order of the Patriotic War. Chinese journalist Hu Jibang (right) exposed the cruelty of the fascist invaders and documented the resilience and courage of the Soviet people as well as their joy during victory.

觉醒的日本士兵俘虏自愿留在抗日根据地，参加反对日本侵略战争的工作。图为他们正在制作装有传单和食品的慰问袋。

Reformed Japanese prisoners packed gift bags with leaflets and food.
A number of Japanese prisoners of war voluntarily stayed back in the CPC-led resistance base areas where they joined Chinese people's efforts to oppose the war of aggression waged by Japanese militarists.

同盟同袍

Allies
in Arms

跨越国界的生死盟约
Transnational Covenants of Life and Death

　　中国人民抗日战争为世界反法西斯战争的胜利作出了巨大的民族牺牲和历史性贡献，同时也得到国际社会的广泛同情和大力支持。苏联给予中国抗战有力的物资支持，美国"飞虎队"冒险开辟驼峰航线，朝鲜、越南、加拿大、印度、新西兰、波兰、丹麦以及德国、奥地利、罗马尼亚、保加利亚、日本等国的一大批反法西斯战士直接投身中国抗战。

　　中国人民抗日战争胜利是中国人民同反法西斯同盟国以及各国人民并肩战斗的伟大胜利。中国人民永远不会忘记，世界上爱好和平与正义的国家和人民、国际组织等各种反法西斯力量对中国人民抗日战争给予的宝贵援助和支持。

The Chinese People's War of Resistance Against Japanese Aggression involved tremendous national sacrifices and historic contributions to the World Anti-Fascist War. Their efforts won the Chinese people sympathy and support from many other countries. The Soviet Union provided substantial material support to China, while the U.S. "Flying Tigers" ventured to establish the Hump route, a perilous aerial supply line during WWII. Anti-fascist activists from many countries—Korea, Vietnam, Canada, India, New Zealand, Poland, Denmark, Germany, Austria, Romania, Bulgaria, and even Japan—fought alongside the Chinese people.

The victory of the Chinese People's War of Resistance Against Japanese Aggression stands as a great triumph achieved through the joint struggle of the Chinese people with fellow Allied Forces members and people worldwide. The Chinese people will never forget the invaluable assistance and steadfast support extended by peace-loving and justice-upholding countries, peoples, international organizations, and all anti-fascist forces across the globe during the arduous resistance.

苏联是首先向中国提供援助的国家。图为装载苏联援华物资的卡车行进在西北公路上。

A fleet of trucks with aid materials provided by the Soviet Union in northwest China.

The Soviet Union was the first country to offer aid to China after the Chinese People's War of Resistance Against Japanese Aggression began.

1937年11月，苏联派出空军志愿队来华参加对日作战。到1941年6月苏德战争爆发前，先后来华的苏联志愿人员有2000多人，其中200多人在中国战场牺牲。图为苏联空军志愿队队员在武汉机场。

Members of the Soviet Volunteer Group at Wuhan Airport in Hubei Province.

In November 1937, the group was sent to China to fight Japanese troops. By the time war broke out between the Soviet Union and Germany in June 1941, more than 2,000 Soviet volunteers had come to China and more than 200 of them laid down their lives.

1941年8月，在美国政府支持下，美国陆军航空队退役军官陈纳德组建中国空军美国志愿援华航空队，即飞虎队，同年12月来华参战。图为飞虎队队员在昆明合影。

Members of the First American Volunteer Group, popularly known as the "Flying Tigers," in Kunming, Yunnan Province.

The group was founded by Claire Lee Chennault, a retired U.S. Army Air Corps officer, under the authorization of President Franklin D. Roosevelt in August 1941. In December of the year, its members arrived in China to take part in the war of resistance against Japanese aggression.

1942年3月，日军占领缅甸首都仰光，运输援华物资的主要通道——滇缅公路被切断。中美被迫共同开辟空中运输航线，即著名的"驼峰航线"。物资经过"驼峰航线"从印度运到中国昆明，再由汽车、马车、人力车运往中国各地。图为在雪峰间穿行的C-47运输机。

A C-47 Skytrain, a military transport aircraft, weaved through snow-clad mountains.

In March 1942, the Yunnan-Burma Road, the key route for transporting aid materials to China, was blocked due to Japanese occupation of Rangoon, capital of Myanmar, then known as Burma. Faced with the dilemma, China developed an air route, popularly known as the Hump, from Kunming to India, with the help of the United States. The supplies arriving in Kunming via this route were distributed all over the country.

1945年8月22日，苏军进入大连，受到市民热烈欢迎。

The Soviet troops were warmly welcomed by citizens in Dalian, Liaoning Province, on August 22, 1945.

中国人民抗日战争得到世界各国爱好和平的人民和团体的广泛同情和支援。1938年5月，世界学生联合会派代表来华考察。图为代表团在延安受到热烈欢迎。

An international student delegation received a warm welcome on arriving in Yan'an in June 1938.
Peace-loving people and organizations all over the world expressed solidarity with China and offered assistance to the country's resistance against Japanese aggression.

国际反侵略运动大会是一个具有广泛影响的国际性群众组织，共有700多个团体会员，代表着4亿以上人口。图为1938年2月，该会在伦敦召开援华大会。

In February 1938, a rally sponsored by the International Peace Campaign in London in support of China's resistance against Japanese aggression.

The campaign was a non-governmental organization with more than 700 member groups representing over 400 million people all over the world.

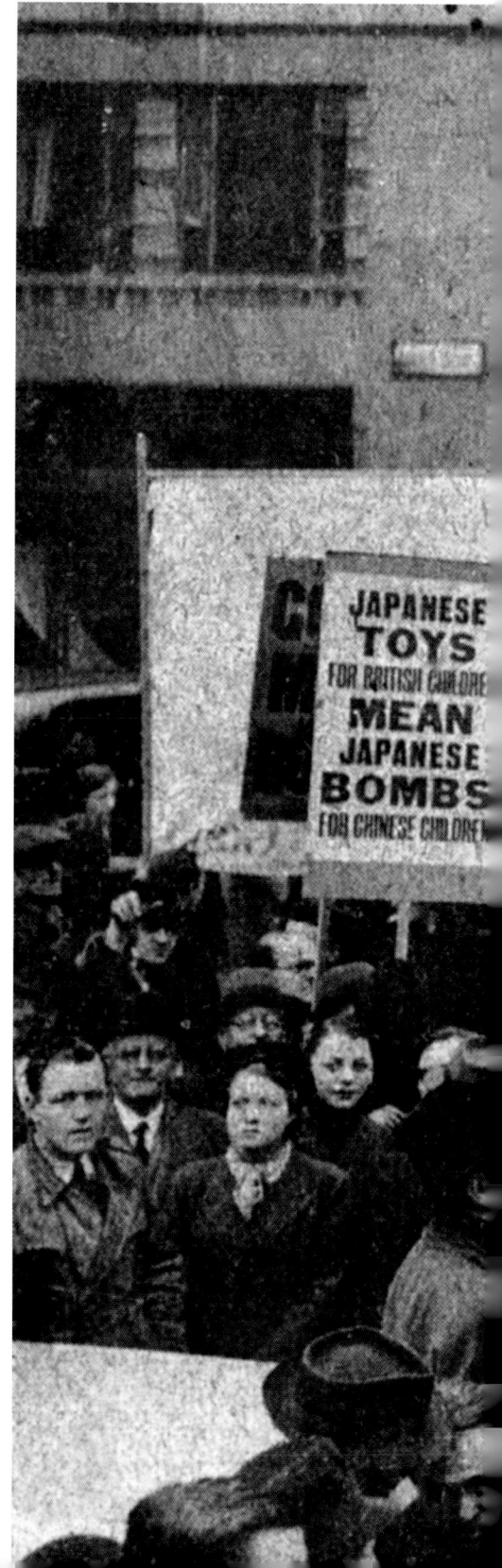

世界各国人民纷纷游行，抗议日本侵略中国。

A march protesting Japanese aggression against China.

在抗日根据地工作的燕京大学经济学教授、英国人林迈可（中）向八路军无线电技术高级训练班的学员们解答问题。

Michael Francis Morris Lindsay (center) taught radio technology to soldiers of the Eighth Route Army at a training class.
The British professor at Yenching University in Beiping (today's Beijing) worked at the CPC-led resistance base areas.

"一碗饭运动"，这场支援中国抗战的运动最初由美国医药援华会和旅美华侨团体于1938年在美国发起，号召美国人民将节约"一碗饭"的钱捐给中国抗战。图为美国妇女在"一碗饭运动"宴会上为中国抗战捐款。

An American woman donated money on Rice Bowl Party Night.

The Rice Bowl Program was initially launched in the United States in 1938 by the American Medical Aid Association for China and overseas Chinese organizations to raise funds to assist China's war of resistance against Japanese aggression.

世界各国的新闻工作者纷纷来华，报道中国抗战实况，揭露日本侵略行径，呼吁世界人民了解中国，支持中国。图为台儿庄战役时，外国记者到前线采访。

Foreign reporters on the frontline at Tai'erzhuang, Shandong Province.

Many foreign journalists came to China to report on China's war of resistance against Japanese aggression. They exposed the atrocities of Japanese aggressors and called on people in the rest of the world to understand the situation and support China.

1939年，德国医生汉斯·米勒来到中国，先后在太行山区和延安从事医疗工作。图为米勒（右1）在为病人做透视检查。

Hans Müller (first right) x-rayed a patient.

The German doctor arrived in China in 1939 and offered medical services in the Taihang Mountain region and Yan'an.

1938年3月，加拿大共产党员、外科医生白求恩率医疗队到达延安，不久赴晋察冀边区工作。1939年11月，白求恩在为伤员进行急救手术时受感染，11月12日，在河北唐县病逝。图为白求恩（右1）在前线为八路军伤员做手术。

Norman Bethune (first right) performed emergency battlefield surgery on a wounded soldier of the Eighth Route Army.

In March 1938, Bethune, a Canadian surgeon and member of the Communist Party of Canada, arrived in Yan'an and later worked at the resistance bases in north China. While operating on a soldier in November 1939, Bethune cut his finger and contracted blood poisoning. He died in Tangxian County, Hebei Province, on November 12, 1939.

1937年11月，留在南京的西方人士成立"南京安全区国际委员会"和"国际红十字会南京委员会"，对遭日军疯狂屠杀的南京难民进行了人道主义的保护与救济。图为南京安全区国际委员会主席拉贝（左3）和委员会部分成员。

John Rabe (third left), President of the International Committee for the Nanjing Safety Zone, and some other committee members.

In November 1937, the German businessman and other Western nationals founded the International Committee for the Nanjing Safety Zone and the International Red Cross Committee of Nanjing to provide Chinese survivors of the Japanese massacre with humanitarian protection and relief.

1937年12月初，丹麦人辛德贝格（左）和德国人卡尔·昆德（右），在江南水泥厂参加了保护中国难民的工作。

Danish citizen Bernhard Arp Sindberg (left) and German Karl Gunther (right) helped shelter Chinese refugees at the Jiangnan Cement Factory in Nanjing in early December 1937.

胜利荣光

Glory of Victory

正义对邪恶的审判

Justice's Trial of Evil

经过 14 年不屈不挠的英勇斗争，中国人民打败了穷凶极恶的日本军国主义侵略者，赢得了近代以来中国反抗外敌入侵的第一次完全胜利。

这一伟大胜利，彻底粉碎了日本军国主义殖民奴役中国的图谋，洗刷了近代以来中国抗击外来侵略屡战屡败的民族耻辱。这一伟大胜利，重新确立了中国在世界上的大国地位，中国人民赢得了世界爱好和平人民的尊敬。这一伟大胜利，开辟了中华民族伟大复兴的光明前景，开启了古老中国凤凰涅槃、浴火重生的新征程。这一伟大胜利，也是中国人民为世界反法西斯战争胜利、维护世界和平作出的重大贡献。

After valiantly fighting a bloody war for 14 years, the Chinese people won the first complete victory in their resistance against foreign invasion in modern times.

This great victory smashed the plot of Japanese militarism to enslave China, washed away the Chinese people's humiliation from being repeatedly defeated by foreign invaders in modern times, and re-established China as a major country, winning its people the respect of the peace-loving people all over the world. This great victory ushered in bright prospects for the great rejuvenation of the Chinese nation, marking a new journey of rebirth for time-honored China—a phoenix rising from the ashes. The great victory also represented a significant contribution by the Chinese people to the victory of the World Anti-Fascist War and the safeguarding of global peace.

从1944年起，八路军、新四军普遍向日、伪军展开反攻作战。图为八路军收复河北任丘县城。

The Eighth Route Army took back Renqiu County in Hebei Province from Japanese forces.
From 1944, the Eighth Route Army and the New Fourth Army undertook large-scale counteroffensives.

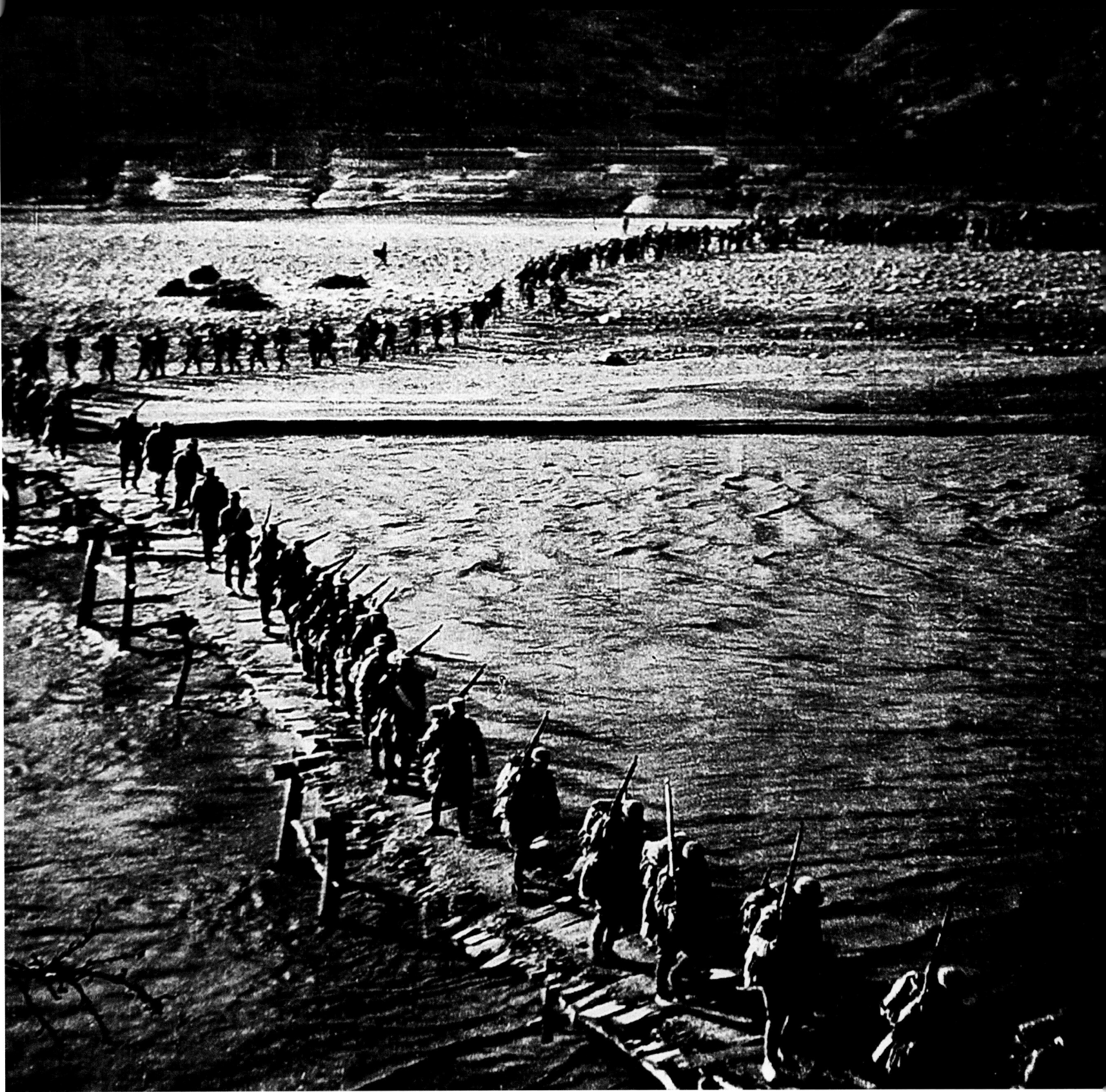

1944年，晋察冀边区八路军渡过滹沱河，向敌占区进军。

In 1944, a branch of Eighth Route Army from the Shanxi-Chahar-Hebei revolutionary base area crossed the Hutuo River and advanced into Japanese-occupied areas.

1945年1月27日，中国远征军、驻印军在缅甸芒友会师，中印公路与滇缅公路贯通，缅北滇西反攻作战取得完全胜利。图为中国远征军、驻印军和盟军在云南畹町举行会师典礼。

Representatives of the Chinese Expeditionary Force, the Chinese troops stationed in India, and the Allied Forces held a joint-force ceremony in Wanding, Yunnan Province.

On January 27, 1945, the Chinese Expeditionary Force and the Chinese troops stationed in India joined forces in Mongyu, Myanmar (then Burma). The Stilwell Road and the Yunnan-Burma Road were connected the same month, marking a complete triumph of the Chinese army's counterattack in north Myanmar and west Yunnan Province.

中国战场对日作战的主战场地位、中国人民的抗战决心和长期抗战行动，使中国反法西斯大国地位得以确立。
1943年1月11日，中美、中英分别在华盛顿和重庆签订平等新约。

On January 11, 1943, China signed equal treaties with the United States and Britain in Washington, D.C. and Chongqing respectively.
China's contribution to WWII as a major theater, the Chinese people's resolve to resist the Japanese aggressors, and their lasting engagement in the war of resistance made China a major force in the World Anti-Fascist War.

1945年4月25日至6月26日，在美国旧金山举行了联合国制宪会议，通过了《联合国宪章》。1945年10月24日，《联合国宪章》生效，联合国正式宣告成立。中国成为联合国安理会常任理事国。图为会议开幕式。

The opening ceremony of the San Francisco Conference in 1945.
From April 25 to June 26, 1945, representatives of 50 countries met in San Francisco, the United States, to draw up the *Charter of the United Nations*. The charter, adopted at the conclusion of the conference, took effect on October 24, 1945, marking the birth of the United Nations. China became a permanent member of the United Nations Security Council.

中国政府代表顾维钧在《联合国宪章》上签字。

V. K. Wellington Koo, a representative of the government of China, signed the *Charter of the United Nations*.

中国政府代表董必武在《联合国宪章》上签字。

Dong Biwu, a representative of the government of China, signed the *Charter of the United Nations*.

1945年7月17日至8月2日，苏、美、英三国在德国柏林附近的波茨坦举行会议。7月26日，会议以美、中、英名义发表敦促日本无条件投降的《波茨坦公告》。苏联对日宣战后，也声明成为公告签署国。

From July 17 to August 2, 1945, leaders of the Soviet Union, the United States and Britain held a conference in Potsdam, Germany. On July 26, the conference issued the *Potsdam Declaration* in the names of the United States, China and Britain, demanding Japan surrender unconditionally. After declaring war on Japan, the Soviet Union also became a signatory to the declaration.

日军向八路军缴械投降。

Japanese soldiers laid down their arms and surrendered to the Eighth Route Army.

1945年8月15日，日本天皇裕仁以广播《终战诏书》的形式，宣布接受《波茨坦公告》。图为关岛的日军战俘在收听广播。

Japanese prisoners of war listened to the radio broadcast of the *Imperial Rescript on Japan's Surrender* on August 15, 1945.
In the broadcast, Japanese Emperor Hirohito announced his country's acceptance of the *Potsdam Declaration*, the July 26 statement which had demanded Japan's unconditional surrender.

1945年9月2日，同盟国与日本在停泊于东京湾的美国密苏里号战列舰上举行日本投降签字仪式。

The ceremony of Japan's surrender was held aboard the U.S. Navy battleship USS Missouri on September 2, 1945. Japan signed the *Japanese Instrument of Surrender* with the Allied Forces.

1945年9月9日，中国战区日军投降签字仪式在原南京国民政府中央军校礼堂举行。

The surrender ceremony of Japanese forces in the China Theater was held in the Central Military School of the former Nanjing National Government on September 9, 1945.

1945年10月25日，中国战区台湾省受降仪式在台北公会堂（今中山堂）举行。遭受日本殖民统治达50年的台湾回到祖国怀抱。

The surrender ceremony of Japanese forces in Taiwan Province of the China Theater was held in Taipei on October 25, 1945. Taiwan, colonized by Japan for 50 years, was returned to China.

延安　Yan'an

台湾　Taiwan

重庆　Chongqing

南京　Nanjing

东北　Northeast China

中国人民欢庆中国人民抗日战争暨世界
反法西斯战争胜利。

The Chinese people celebrated the
victory of the war of resistance and the
World Anti-Fascist War.

1946年5月3日至1948年11月12日，同盟国在东京设立的远东国际军事法庭，审判了东条英机等28名日本甲级战犯。图为远东国际军事法庭。

The International Military Tribunal for the Far East.
From May 3, 1946 to November 12, 1948, the tribunal, set up by the Allied Forces in Tokyo, tried and charged 28 Japanese military and political leaders, including Tojo Hideki, with Class-A crimes.

1946年2月15日，南京审判战犯军事法庭成立，主要审理制造南京大屠杀惨案的日本战犯和其他日本战犯。1946年8月，乙级战犯、南京大屠杀主犯之一谷寿夫被押解至中国；从1947年2月6日起法庭对其进行公审，3月10日判决其死刑。判决书中写明南京大屠杀的受难同胞在30万人以上。图为谷寿夫在法庭上接受审判。

Tani Hisao, one of the principal perpetrators of the Nanjing Massacre, stood on trial at the Nanjing War Crimes Tribunal.

On February 15, 1946, the Nanjing War Crimes Tribunal was established to try Japanese war criminals responsible for the Nanjing Massacre and other atrocities. In August 1946, Tani Hisao, a Class B war criminal, was extradited to China. The tribunal conducted public trials from February 6 to March 10, 1947, ultimately sentencing Tani Hisao to death for his role in the massacre. The trial transcripts explicitly state that the number of victims of the Nanjing Massacre exceeded 300,000.

1949年12月，在苏联伯力城由苏联滨海军区军事法庭公开审判了侵华日军七三一部队制造细菌武器的战犯。图为法庭内景。

War criminals from Unit 731 of the Japanese army were brought to trial at a Soviet military court in Khabarovsk, the Soviet Union, in December 1949.

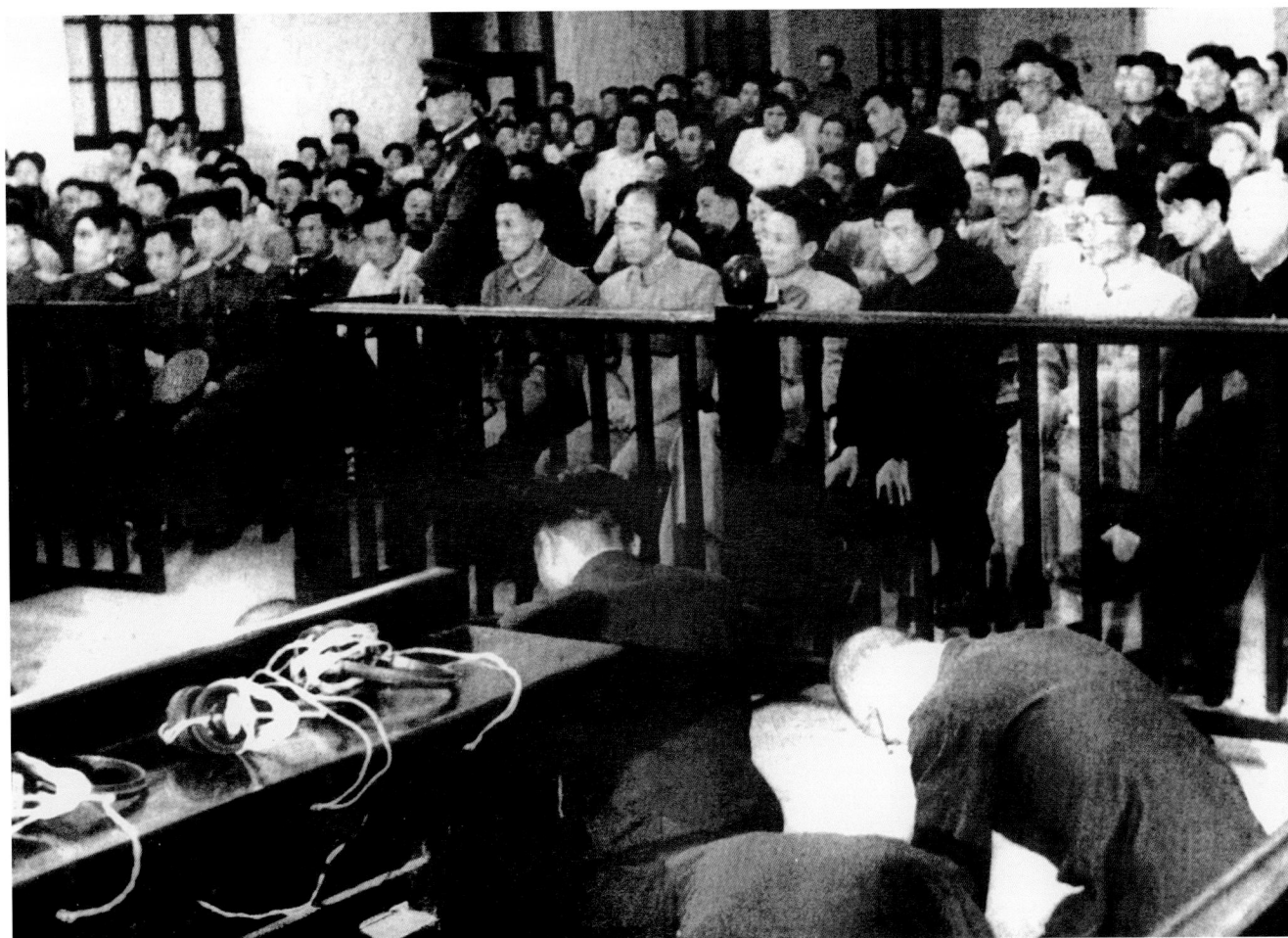

1956年6月至7月，中华人民共和国最高人民法院特别军事法庭在沈阳和太原两地，公开审判了45名日本战犯。图为日本战犯在法庭上跪地谢罪。

Japanese war criminals knelt down to apologize for their atrocities in a court of the Special Military Tribunal of the Supreme People's Court of the People's Republic of China.

From June to July 1956, the tribunal publicly brought 45 Japanese war criminals to trial in Shenyang, Liaoning Province, and Taiyuan, Shanxi Province.

青史长铭

Eternal
Memories

永恒的和平守望

Timeless Pursuit of Peace

历史的记忆和真相不会随着岁月流逝而褪色，带给我们的启迪永远映照现实、昭示未来。我们要以史为鉴，从第二次世界大战的深刻教训和反法西斯战争的伟大胜利中汲取智慧和力量，坚决反对一切形式的霸权主义和强权政治，共同创造人类更加美好的未来。

铭记历史，不是为了延续仇恨，而是要引以为戒。传承历史，不是为了纠结过去，而是要开创未来，让和平薪火代代相传。80 年前，我们经过奋起反抗，赢得了反法西斯战争伟大胜利。80 年后的今天，我们要采取一切必要措施，坚决维护自身主权、安全、发展利益，坚定做历史记忆的守护者、发展振兴的同行者、国际公平正义的捍卫者，携手为人类前途命运争取更加光明的未来。

Historical memory and truth never fade with the passage of time; they continually illuminate our present and guide our future. We must consider history a mirror and draw wisdom and strength from the profound lessons of WWII and the great victory of the World Anti-Fascist War. We resolutely oppose all forms of hegemonism and power politics, and advocate working together to create a brighter future for humanity.

Remembering history is not to perpetuate hatred, but to learn for the future. Inheriting history is not to dwell on the past, but to forge ahead and pass on the torch of peace from generation to generation. Eight decades ago, through resolute resistance, we achieved a great victory in the World Anti-Fascist War. Today, as we commemorate this milestone, we must take all necessary measures to resolutely safeguard our sovereignty, security, and development interests. We stand firm as guardians of historical memory, partners in development, and defenders of international fairness and justice. Let us join hands to secure a brighter future for humanity.

遇难者名单墙
Wall of Victims' List
犠 牲 者 名 簿 の 壁

参观由此向前
Visit forward from here

侵华日军南京大屠杀遇难同胞纪念馆序厅的遇难者名单墙上镌刻着1万余名被认定的遇难者姓名，被人们称作"哭墙"。由于南京大屠杀中的遇难者往往没有尸体，没有坟墓，"哭墙"成为不少遗属们祭奠亲人的唯一寄托。

The names of more than 10,000 identified victims are engraved on the wall in the foyer of the Memorial Hall of the Victims in Nanjing Massacre by Japanese Invaders, which is called the "Wailing Wall." As the bodies of victims of the Nanjing Massacre were seldom found and lack graves, the "Wailing Wall" has become the only place for many bereaved families to mourn their loved ones killed in the massacre.

著名雕塑家吴为山创作的《侵华日军南京大屠杀遇难同胞纪念馆扩建工程组雕》之《逃难之三——孤儿》：飞机又来轰炸了！失去双亲的孤儿在惊吓与恐惧中携手逃生。

Escape No. 3—Orphan, created by famous sculptor Wu Weishan, is part of the group sculptures for the expansion project of the Memorial Hall of the Victims in Nanjing Massacre by Japanese Invaders. This sculpture presents a scene of orphans fleeing in fright during a Japanese air raid.

133

云南龙陵县，云龙山半山腰上的抗战胜利纪念碑承载了龙陵几代人对中国远征军的缅怀与崇敬。

The monument to the victory of the Chinese People's War of Resistance Against Japanese Aggression on Yunlong Mountain in Longling County, Yunnan Province, carries local people's respect for the Chinese Expeditionary Force.

2014年5月4日，由日本全国保险医团联合会和全日本民主医疗机关联合会组成的26人代表团参观侵华日军第七三一部队罪证陈列馆。

A 26-member delegation from the All-Japan Federation of National Health Insurance Organizations and the Japan Federation of Democratic Medical Institutions visited the Exhibition Hall of Evidences of Crime Committed by Unit 731 of the Japanese Imperial Army in Harbin, Heilongjiang Province, on May 4, 2014.

2015年9月3日，纪念中国人民抗日战争暨世界反法西斯战争胜利70周年阅兵式在天安门广场举行。10时41分，空中护旗方队率先亮相，揭开阅兵分列式的序幕——两架直升机分别悬挂中华人民共和国国旗和中国人民解放军军旗飞过天安门广场，直升机群在空中组成"70"字样。

A military parade celebrating the 70th anniversary of the victory of the Chinese People's War of Resistance Against Japanese Aggression and the World Anti-Fascist War was held at the Tian'anmen Square on September 3, 2015. At 10:41 a.m., an air echelon escorting the national flag of the People's Republic of China and the flag of the Chinese People's Liberation Army (PLA) flew over the Tian'anmen Square, followed by a helicopter group forming the number "70" in the air, marking the start of the parade.

2015

2015年9月3日，北京，纪念中国人民抗日战争暨世界反法西斯战争胜利70周年阅兵式上，330余名抗战老战士、抗日英烈子女和抗战支前模范代表组成的老兵方阵，在国宾护卫队的护卫下，乘敞篷车徐徐驶来，率先通过天安门广场。

A phalanx composed of more than 330 veterans, models in supporting the front, and relatives of the martyrs in the Chinese People's War of Resistance Against Japanese Aggression, escorted by a state guest motorcade, passed through the Tian'anmen Square in open-top minibuses at a military parade commemorating the 70th anniversary of the victory of the Chinese People's War of Resistance Against Japanese Aggression and the World Anti-Fascist War in Beijing on September 3, 2015.

2018年9月1日，南京，侵华日军南京大屠杀遇难同胞纪念馆，人们驻足在李自健的巨幅油画作品《南京大屠杀——屠·生·佛》前。

Visitors viewed Li Zijian's large oil painting *Nanjing Massacre—Slaughter, Life, and Buddha* at the Memorial Hall of the Victims in Nanjing Massacre by Japanese Invaders on September 1, 2018.

2020年9月3日，沈阳"九·一八"历史博物馆举行"铭记历史 开创未来 众馆联动 守望和平"中国人民抗日战争暨世界反法西斯战争胜利75周年主题活动。

The 9·18 Historical Museum in Shenyang held an event alongside other museums commemorating the 75th anniversary of the victory of the Chinese People's War of Resistance Against Japanese Aggression and World Anti-Fascist War on September 3, 2020.

2020年9月3日，上海，中国人民抗日战争暨世界反法西斯战争胜利75周年纪念日。不少市民游客在参观完四行仓库抗战纪念馆后，纷纷来到馆外的晋元纪念广场弹孔墙前献花或摆上一份祭品，悼念在抗战中英勇牺牲的先烈。

September 3, 2020 marked the 75th anniversary of the victory of the Chinese People's War of Resistance Against Japanese Aggression and the World Anti-Fascist War. On that day, after visiting the Shanghai Sihang Warehouse Battle Memorial, many people visited the "bullet ridden" wall at the Jinyuan Memorial Square outside the museum to lay flowers or offer tributes, mourning the soldiers who sacrificed their lives in the war.

2023年9月3日，沈阳，中国人民抗日战争暨世界反法西斯战争胜利78周年纪念日之际，民众参观"九·一八"历史博物馆。

On September 3, 2023, the 78th anniversary of the victory of the Chinese People's War of Resistance Against Japanese Aggression and the World Anti-Fascist War, people visited the 9·18 Historical Museum in Shenyang City.

2024年9月3日，北京，"四海同歌——纪念中国人民抗日战争暨世界反法西斯战争胜利79周年"主题音乐会在中国人民抗日战争纪念馆举行。

A concert commemorating the 79th anniversary of the victory of the Chinese People's War of Resistance Against Japanese Aggression and the World Anti-Fascist War was held at the Museum of the War of Chinese People's Resistance Against Japanese Aggression in Beijing on September 3, 2024.

2024年9月3日，中国人民抗日战争暨世界反法西斯战争胜利79周年纪念日，"铭记英雄——飞虎队主题历史图片展巡展"开展仪式暨征集美国籍抗日航空英烈信息发布仪式在南京抗日航空烈士纪念馆举行，展出了近180张珍贵历史图片和70余件文物史料。图为参加图片展的中外人士向抗日航空烈士纪念碑默哀。

Chinese and foreign participants in the "Remembering Heroes—Flying Tigers" Themed Historical Photo Exhibition Tour paid a silent tribute to the Anti-Japanese Aviation Martyrs Monument.

September 3, 2024 was the 79th anniversary of the victory of the Chinese People's War of Resistance Against Japanese Aggression and World Anti-Fascist War. The photo exhibition tour and an event for collecting information on American anti-Japanese aviation heroes were launched at the Memorial Hall of Nanjing Anti-Japanese Aviation Martyrs. The exhibition displayed nearly 180 precious historical photos and more than 70 cultural relics and historical materials.

2024年3月8日，安徽马鞍山，抗战老兵向新兵讲述战斗故事。

A veteran of the Chinese People's War of Resistance Against Japanese Aggression recounted stories of his wartime experiences to young troops in Ma'anshan City, Anhui Province, on March 8, 2024.

2025年4月17日，浙江衢州，"我们衢州见"中美民间友好交流活动举行，"杜立特行动"大救援参与村民后裔廖明发（前排右）向美中航空遗产基金会副主席、美国飞虎队成员后裔克利福德·雷·朗（Clifford Ray Long Jr.）展示老照片。

Liao Mingfa (front, right), a descendant of villagers who participated in the rescue of the Doolittle Raiders, showed old photos to Clifford Ray Long Jr., vice chairman of the Sino-American Aviation Heritage Foundation and a descendant of a member of the American "Flying Tigers." The "See You in Quzhou" China-U.S. People-to-People Exchange event was held on April 17, 2025, in Quzhou City, Zhejiang Province.

当地时间2025年5月9日，俄罗斯首都莫斯科，中国人民解放军三军仪仗队方队参加纪念苏联伟大卫国战争胜利80周年阅兵式。

The guard of honor of the PLA's Army, Navy, and Air Force joined a parade in Moscow, the capital of Russia, on May 9, 2025, commemorating the 80th anniversary of the victory in the Soviet Union's Great Patriotic War.

图书在版编目（CIP）数据

和平的丰碑：纪念中国人民抗日战争暨世界反法西
斯战争胜利 80 周年：汉英对照 / 人民画报编著；殷星，
刘海乐，周昕译 . -- 北京：新世界出版社，2025.8.
ISBN 978-7-5104-8195-6

Ⅰ . K265.07-64

中国国家版本馆 CIP 数据核字第 2025PQ9281 号

和平的丰碑
——纪念中国人民抗日战争暨世界反法西斯战争胜利 80 周年（汉英对照）

作　　者：人民画报

策　　划：于　佳　朱　芳

责任编辑：赵如意

图文统筹：黄丽巍

英文翻译：殷　星　刘海乐　周　昕

责任校对：宣　慧　张杰楠

装帧设计：迟　森

责任印制：王宝根

图片支持：中国人民抗日战争纪念馆　中国专题图库
　　　　　视觉中国　山东广播电视台

出　　版：新世界出版社

网　　址：http://www.nwp.com.cn

社　　址：北京西城区百万庄大街 24 号 （100037）

发 行 部：(010)6899 5968 （电话） (010)6899 0635 （电话）

总 编 室：(010)6899 5424 （电话） (010)6832 6679 （传真）

版 权 部：+8610 6899 6306 （电话） nwpcd@sina.com （电邮）

印　　刷：小森印刷（北京）有限公司

经　　销：新华书店

开　　本：889mm×1194mm 1/12　尺寸：285mm×280mm

字　　数：100 千字　印张：13.5

版　　次：2025 年 8 月第 1 版　2025 年 8 月第 1 次印刷

书　　号：ISBN 978-7-5104-8195-6

定　　价：358.00 元